Direct Mail
Success

To David, Roger, and Julie

Glenn
Bridge
Press

St. Louis, Missouri • Clearwater, Florida

Direct Mail
Success

Great Ideas, Proven Strategies,
and Practical Techniques

by *Gil Effron*

Foreword by
Mike Panaggio

Published in the U.S.A. by
Glenn Bridge Press
ISBN 0-9657918-1-5

Library of Congress Catalog Card Number: 00-090623

Effron, Gil
    1. Direct mail strategies and techniques
    2. Direct mail planning
    3. Direct mail implementaion

This publication is designed to provide accurate and authoritative information regarding the subject matter covered. The publisher is not engaged in rendering legal, accounting or other professional service. If legal advice or other expert assistance is required, the services of a competent professional should be sought.

Printed in the U.S.A.

10 9 8 7 6 5 4 3 2

Foreword

by *Mike Panaggio*

Shortly after Jorge Villar, Phil Turk, and I founded Response Mail Express in 1995, the first edition of *Direct Mail Success* crossed my desk. I read it all in one day. This simple, little compendium of direct mail ideas, strategies, and techniques reaffirmed *everything* we believed in when it came to deploying effective direct mail.

Even today, whenever I sense that our own direct marketing strategy sessions might be heading in the wrong direction, I pull out my now dog-eared first edition, with all its marginal scribbles and notes, and go back to the basics.

And as often as I personally refer to a chapter here or there, I refer one of our customers to specific ideas regarding copy, design, premiums, pricing strategies, and so on. The reason is simple: Time after time, *Direct Mail Success* provides the fundamentals of direct mail — the strategies, tactics, and techniques every mailer needs to increase response. In fact, Gil Effron's unwavering attitude toward simplicity and his "get it in the mail now!" philosophy are what we ourselves use daily to help thousands of companies deploy professional, effective direct mail.

The creative process is important. As Gil says, "Without it, the direct marketing industry would be lost." However, as Gil also points out, the creative process can be "a *black hole*" where would-be direct mail tycoons enter, never to return. The problem with the creative process is that it requires *time.* When a company is planning, talking, deciding, thinking, and deliberating *what* to do, it can lose valuable selling time. If it takes several months to develop a direct mail campaign, that means several months of lost sales.

Case in point. Several years ago, I had the opportunity to share *Direct Mail Success* and the Response Mail Express story with a prospect — the president of a computer software firm in Orlando, Florida. During the course of our meeting, he showed me at least half a dozen direct mail ideas that he, his staff, and his creative team had *talked* about doing during the past year. However, none had made it into the mail. "We couldn't take the chance of mailing the *wrong* thing," he said. "So, we didn't mail anything. We kept hoping that the next new idea that came along would convince us to take a leap of faith and make the financial investment."

I pointed out the black hole of direct mail planning and showed him how the creative process was actually getting in the way of his success. Then I showed him several of our unique and innovative stock programs. And I shared with him the success that thousands of companies in hundreds of industries have enjoyed as a result of using one or more of our pre-designed and pre-printed stock direct mail formats.

In about half an hour, he and I selected a design format, looked at some proven copy alternatives, considered a premium offer, and shook hands. Three days later, Response Mail Express had him in the mail. Within a week, the phones were ringing and he was writing new business.

Throughout the years — by combining the tried and true techniques of *Direct Mail Success* with the proven, high-impact stock mailing programs from Response Mail Express — we have helped him to be able to mail more frequently, to attain a predictably higher response rate, and to see greater long-term success in his entire direct mail program. And we have accomplished the same for thousands upon thousands of other companies.

Where to begin? If you read only two chapters in this book, I recommend two. The first, "The Creative Abyss," *Page 32,* deals with this very dilemma. The second critical section, "When You Can't Predict Response Rate," *Page 40,* talks about how to calculate the effectiveness of a mailing program. These are two basic ideas that we utilize continually — thanks to Gil Effron. He keeps us on target.

> *Mike Panaggio*
> *Response Mail Express*
> *A division of DME*
> *Tampa, Florida*
> *April 30, 2000*

Contents

Section 3 :
Direct Mail Design

Section 4 :
Creating Effective Direct Mail Copy

Section 5 :
Mailing Lists and Personalized Mail

Section 6 :
Sales and Pricing Strategies

Introduction

Whether you are brand new to direct mail or a seasoned direct mail veteran, our hope is that *Direct Mail Success* points the way toward maximizing your direct mail effectiveness.

To that end, we are pleased to provide you with hundreds of great ideas, proven direct mail strategies, and practical implementation techniques.

You may find it helpful to start at the beginning and read straight through, or pick out those titles that seem most relevant.

Either way, keep this book close at hand — to spark ideas that help you develop better overall direct mail strategies, to find new ways to motivate your readers and prospects into action, to improve response, to develop better-looking direct mail graphics, and to help you keep your data fresh, current, and valuable.

Our hope is that you find some thought-provoking ideas that you can put to work *today* to increase your mailing effectiveness *tomorrow*.

A Rationale For Direct Mail

Direct Mail:
A Measurable Medium

Direct mail is the most reliable and productive way to reach, motivate, and sell to a specific, qualified audience. In the 1980s, direct mail proved itself as a science. This science showed that by developing the proper offer, packaging it skillfully, and putting it in front of the right prospect, there was a statistical probability that it would be seen, considered, and acted upon.

But there was more. This new science went on to change some base-line thinking in business and industry regarding the cost of advertising and promotion. Instead of looking at "cost per thousand," the direct mail industry demonstrated the importance of measuring "cost per response" when trying to gauge the value of effective promotion. Since direct mail is the only advertising medium that is fully focused, response and cost per response are totally measurable and identifiable factors.

Across the board, targeted marketing that is driven by cost per response has changed the way business and industry think about spending their advertising dollars. While it has its place, the shotgun approach to marketing and advertising claimed by newspapers, magazines, television, and radio may be more *miss* than *hit*. However, direct mail marketing puts you right on the mark.

Direct Mail Requires Professional Support

Direct mail looks easy enough. You print a mailing indicia in the upper-right-hand corner, get some rubber bands, trays and tags, and have at it. But should direct mail really be a do-it-yourself activity?

The answer is an absolute and emphatic, "No!" Preparing mail properly has always been tough, but now it is tougher than ever thanks to the postal reclassification.

Without the professional services of a direct mail company, you run the risk of losing valuable time and considerable money by trying to tackle the job yourself. Today, efficient, accurate, and deliverable direct mail requires up-to-the-minute knowledge of mailing costs, mailing list hygiene, proper formats, automation discounts, carrier routes, bar codes, and much more.

Think about this: You can justify spending a little more to print on a better paper in order to make your mailing look better, or to use a colorful envelope so that it will not be missed. But the quality of postal delivery does not get better or faster just because you *inadvertently* pay more for postage, or because you are not familiar with the ins-and-outs of the postal system. Since postage costs can account for half of your entire direct mail budget — and sometimes more — why would you ever want to spend more than you have to?

Direct mail is a science that professional direct mail companies work with everyday. That makes them experts. Just as they do not profess to be experts at the technology or body of knowledge that you work with in your business, you should not assume that you can do what they do with equal expertise. They do the most good for those clients who put their trust in them, who turn to them as the direct mail experts, and who allow them to show them the *big picture*.

Why distract yourself from what you do best in your business to handle the myriad of details involved in getting your direct mail campaign to the post office when support is so close at hand?

Understanding Where Your Direct Mail Dollar Goes

Anyone who has ever sliced a "direct mail pie" knows that it seems like everyone wants a big piece. In other words, direct mail can be an expensive investment.

The first slice has to go to the post office for postage. The next piece is saved for the printer to cover press time, paper, plates, film, stitching, trimming, and so on.

Then, the creative team — whose work includes planning, copywriting, design, producing artwork, typesetting, and photography — gets a slice for all of its contributions. And, finally, the direct mail service is served for managing the data, folding, inserting, sorting, collating, tabbing, transporting, and a whole lot more.

When some people look at all of the costs associated with this pie, they try to find ways to save money, perhaps to slice the pieces just a little thinner. Sure you can save a little here or a little there, but where in the pie can you save enough to make a difference?

After all, postage rates are nonnegotiable, and you

certainly do not want to compromise the quality of your piece by skimping on the creative or printing aspects. Neither do you want your solicitation to appear less than perfect by cutting corners on presentation and delivery by asking less of your direct mail service.

Any way you cut it, you simply have a lot of costs to cover. Instead of focusing on what you have to *spend*, look at the potential dollars you can *earn* on your investment. A carefully planned and executed direct mail program can mean a significant response from potential customers. That increased response will translate into sales and profits.

When you slice the direct mail pie carefully, but generously, the return will more than satisfy your appetite for increased sales and higher profits.

Direct Mail:
A Silent Powerhouse

The good news is that advertisements in printed publications reach a lot of people.

The bad news is that many of the most avid readers of these printed publications are your toughest, meanest, most aggressive competitors. When they read your ad, it does not take them long to figure out exactly what you are offering, at what price, for how long, and at what specific terms. Everything is right out in the open.

Direct mail advertising provides lots of privacy — more than any other medium. The "silence is golden" nature of direct mail keeps your competitors in the dark and increases the amount of "private time" you have in the marketplace without seeing a response from your competition. No one knows your business except you, and, of course, your prospects and customers.

Additionally, when you run a print ad, you never really know whether or not your prospect received your offer. However, direct mail can be targeted to the right prospect, and it can be perfectly timed to be delivered exactly when you need it to arrive.

Direct mail offers considerable flexibility that other mediums do not. In a newspaper or trade advertisement, everyone gets and reads the same offer — the same deal. You cannot run two different ads with two different offers side by side.

With direct mail, messages can be tailored to address different market segments. Your bigger buyers can get a different message than your smaller buyers, or your fast-to-pay buyers can get better terms than those who do not pay so fast.

The privacy, flexibility, and market targetability of direct mail advertising assure that your advertising dollars are being spent in the best possible way.

Email versus Direct Mail

These days you hear a lot of talk about the Internet, World Wide Web and email, and how they are likely to replace all other forms of mail and direct communication. Some people predict that the speed and accessibility of electronic communications will make paper communications a thing of the past.

The predictions are familiar. Way back when, the daily newspapers feared their demise when they saw that this new contraption called radio could deliver news nearly instantaneously. And many people were once concerned that television would put Hollywood and the motion picture industry out of business.

But, like the newspapers that continue to be printed, and Hollywood, which is thriving thanks to television, paper communications will continue to be an important part of our daily lives. The likelihood that reliable, highly targeted, ink-on-paper direct mail will retreat submissively or be vaporized into cyberspace as a result of the Internet and email is extremely remote.

The reasons are simple. First, direct mail is absolutely targetable, and the industry as a whole improves its ability to target more precisely every day.

Second, mail is proactive. You can wait all year for someone to find you on the Internet or World Wide Web. But your ink-on-paper direct mail offer — at *your* command, instruction, and direction — finds its way directly to your prospect's door.

Additionally, mail does not need RAM, megabytes, or modems. It does not require a knowledge or understanding of computers. If you have a mailbox and know where it is, chances are you get mail.

Finally, mail gives you something tangible, something you can hold in your hand. It gives you something substantial to get excited about or to hang on the refrigerator door for inspiration — to work a little harder and a lot longer.

The Internet, World Wide Web, and email will certainly have their rightful places in effective, modern communications, but history repeats itself. Like newspapers and motion pictures, direct mail is here to stay, because for many situations, direct mail remains the most efficient and most cost-effective means of getting a relevant sales message to a qualified prospect and obtaining direct response.

Weigh Cost of Mailing
Against Value of Results

When it comes to developing a direct mail campaign, it is easy to get trapped into thinking that the only important question to ask of a direct mail company is, "How much (or actually 'how little') will the mailing promotion cost?" It is easy to believe that a lower price is better.

The fact is that what a direct mail piece costs to produce, print, and mail is not always the only or best barometer to consider. The primary consideration really ought to be results.

If you are bold and brave enough to start from a premise that when it comes to direct mail, "price is no object," and you produce direct mail materials based on what you want to achieve in results, you may be pleasantly surprised with the results.

Doing a better job doesn't mean doubling or tripling how much you spend or adopting a "sky's the limit" attitude. If you are willing to spend just a little more on a better design and better copy, your ability to attract more prospects may improve.

If you invest in a slightly better mailing list, you may be able to reach some key prospects you might otherwise have missed. The best kind of prospects are, you know, the ones who buy.

If you spend a little extra for personalizing the sales letter, you might be able to entice someone who ordinarily would not give it the time of day to read every word.

Look at the level of sophistication of the mail that comes to your doorstep these days — both at home and at the office. High-quality mail attracts your attention, and attracting attention means getting your message across.

Don't focus on the cost of the mailing. Instead, look at the expenditure in relation to the increased results you can achieve by investing a little more.

Proven Direct Mail Strategies

Consistent Response Comes From Mailing Consistently

Ever notice how few responses a company receives when it doesn't mail anything?

That may sound like a silly question since it is fairly obvious that if a company doesn't mail, it shouldn't expect to see any response. Conversely, a company that *does* mail can generate tremendous response.

Surprisingly, though, many companies and business owners don't see this cause and effect relationship. Clearly, by sending direct mail to your customers and prospects, you are taking control of your own corporate destiny.

So, here is the corollary: If you mail every day, you are likely to receive responses every day. Likewise, if you mail every week or every month, you are likely to obtain responses every week or every month. The cycle creates itself.

If, for example, you need 20 leads a week for your business, and you know that by mailing 1,000 solicitations a week you generate those 20 leads, then it makes sense to mail 1,000 pieces *every* week.

The problem is that it is easy to get sidetracked. For instance, when business is very good, there is a temptation to stop mailing — at least until the production department gets "caught up." Often, there's too much "other" activity going on — proposals to write, follow-ups from last month, or even the annual sales meeting. (Ever notice how few *new* sales occur during those weeks when a company holds its annual sales meeting?)

But what happens when the proposals finally get written, all the loose ends from last month are tied up, and the sales meeting is finally over? If you have not tried to generate new leads, none will be coming in, and no new leads means no new sales.

By mailing every day, every week or every month, a company can be in constant touch with a meaningful portion of its total market, both customers and prospects. Through a consistent mailing program, each sales lead arrives when it is needed, which minimizes the peaks and valleys that often appear to dominate a company's sales activities.

You know from experience that when you lose a day, there is just no way to go back and do it again (at least not in our time zone). Or, when you lose a month, it is gone for good, along with all the sales, leads, or inquiries associated with it. Suddenly, you have to work a lot harder to make up what you have lost.

Consistency, whether that means mailing every day, every week or every month, is the one key to direct mail success — and to the success of your business. If you like the idea of never losing a day, week or month again, along with all the sales, orders and inquiries that go with it, work toward developing and maintaining a consistent mailing schedule.

The Creative Abyss

The creative process is important. Without it, the direct marketing industry would be lost. After all, ideas move people. And truly creative ideas can move people a lot.

However, the creative process is also a *black hole* where unwary, would-be direct marketing moguls enter — never to return. The problem with the creative process is that it requires *time* — lots of time! Not only that, it is complex. The lengthy process includes a wide range of creative and time-consuming activities, from concept, strategy and planning, to dozens of specific details pertaining to production, printing, data selection and management, mailing, and so on.

So, when companies are planning, talking, deciding, thinking and deliberating *what* to do, they lose valuable selling time. If it takes them two or three months to develop and launch a direct mail campaign, that's two or three *irretrievable* months of lost sales. Once lost, there is no getting it back: not a month, not six, not a year.

Often companies procrastinate when it comes to

deploying a direct mail campaign because they are afraid of doing the *wrong* thing. With good reason. After all, doing the wrong thing can be expensive. However, if doing the *wrong* thing is expensive, consider how expensive it is to do *nothing.*

One way to eliminate the effect of the creative abyss is to start small. A simple, yet well-conceived mailing program such as a fold-over postcard, a traditional sales letter with a business reply card, or a simple flyer is often a whole lot better than a grand plan of nothing. There's still a creative process. However, it's a whole lot more manageable.

Or, you can look to pre-designed and pre-printed stock direct mail formats. Companies such as Response Mail Express of Tampa, Florida, help to bypass the perplexing creative process, because the creative work is already engineered and in place. In addition, these programs often come with a proven track record of success.

Whether you implement something simple on your own or seek out and employ a stock program, the goal is: *Get it in the mail now!* There is no other way to achieve direct mail success.

Test to Learn

Test! Test! Test! You hear this all the time. The fact is, you can never stop testing. If you do, you almost guarantee that your business will never improve. Or, if you stop changing things and leave them as they are, things cannot improve.

But testing is expensive, so be sure you are testing relevant issues. Testing a price point of $59 versus $69 is a worthy cause because it may make you ten bucks richer. And comparing methods of payment is potentially a valuable inquiry. Even evaluating the predominance of phone responses instead of business-reply cards may present some interesting data.

Since testing can be expensive, make sure to minimize error in your testing. It is important to test only one element at a time. If you test price point and method of payment simultaneously, you may never really know what the results mean. Your test can be invalidated simply because you cannot identify which of your variables had the most impact.

The results you get from testing, give you the confidence

to implement changes that will improve your overall response. With well-planned testing, you begin to develop specific performance data on each individual test you conduct. The bottom line is that there is no pass or fail in this kind of testing. You can only use the knowledge and insight you have gained to see a better response each time you mail.

The Easy Way to Master Postal Regulations

It weighs six pounds, twelve ounces and has a 22-page table of contents. The first time you read a paragraph, you ask yourself, "Did I miss something?" So, you read it again. It sounds logical enough, like it *should* make sense. But it does not. See for yourself:

"Package (or bundle) preparation is intended to present a mailing sorted to at least the finest extent required by the standards for the rate claimed. Generally, package (or bundle) presort is from the lowest (finest) to the highest level, to those destinations specified by standard and is completed at each level before the next level is prepared."

That paragraph comes right from the *United States Postal Service Domestic Mail Manual.* It tells you what you can and cannot do when it comes to processing direct mail. And, quite frankly, it can be overwhelming, even boring.

Believe it or not, though, direct mail professionals like this book. They *really* like it. They read it all the time, sometimes every day. They are able to make heads and tails out of it, not just that one paragraph, but every paragraph in the entire manual.

The good news is that because they are the experts at reading and working their way through the *Domestic Mail Manual* and every aspect of bulk-mail preparation, you do not have to be.

Because they know the rules and regulations inside and out, you never have to read a single page in that perplexing postal manual. Instead, you can focus on your business — selling more, talking to customers more, and making more money.

Most importantly, using a professional, direct mail company ensures that you never spend a penny more than you have to on postage and mailing. When it comes to your mail, the goal of a professional direct mail company is to make your life *easy*.

Always Ask for a
Specific Response

If you never ask her to marry you, you will always be single.
It is true. No matter how much you say you love her, no matter how much you spend on candy or flowers, no matter what gifts you bestow upon her, you will always be single unless you eventually pop the question, "Will you marry me?"

Direct mail advertising is a lot like proposing.

Unless you ask your prospects to buy, they will never buy. Unless you ask your readers to respond, they will never respond. Unless you ask your customers to call, they will never call. Unless you ask for the order, you will never get it.

This popping of the question is what we call the "call to action." It is what gives direct mail a strategic advantage over most other advertising mediums. It establishes the inherent ability to provide a measurable response to a specific offer at a specific point in time.

A good salesman, one-on-one with his prospect, must

ask for the sale, or it will never happen. This is his call to action and his way to measure his personal effectiveness. This same advantage always exists with direct mail.

By simply popping the question or asking for a response, you get to tap into the powerful advantage of direct mail. When you do, you will see that direct mail is just like proposing. Well, except that the honeymoon is a little different.

When You Can't Predict Response Rate

Imagine having a crystal ball that predicts your direct mail response rate. Wouldn't it be nice to know exactly what your return on your investment will be before you mail?

Unfortunately, crystal balls are unreliable, and there is no such thing as a guaranteed response rate. In fact, predicting any kind of a response rate is difficult, if not impossible, because countless variables can affect your response. Just to list a few:

- Your price
- The mailing list you select
- Your creative approach
- The offer
- The uniqueness of your product
- Your competitor's price
- The seasonality of your product or offer
- The image you project
- Mother Nature

Still, you need something tangible on which to base your decisions. One possibility is to determine a *break-even point*, and then to evaluate the likelihood that you will sell enough to reach it. The following simple model explains the break-even approach.

If your new item retails for $100 and costs you $50 to buy or build, that leaves $50 to cover your overhead and the cost of your promotion. Suppose your direct mail program — including mailing list, printing, production, and mailing services — costs $400 per thousand pieces. Divide the $400 per thousand by the $50 gross profit, which equals eight units per one thousand mail pieces. These eight units represent the number of sales you need in order to break even (before overhead).

Selling eight units for every one thousand pieces mailed is .008 percent (8/10 of one percent) — just under a percentage point. Now, based on what you know about your company, the industry and the product, does that closing ratio seem realistic and attainable?

Next, ask yourself whether you can really sell eight units for every thousand pieces that you mail. To arrive at an answer, look at similar products and customer buying trends. If your current customers always buy two at a time, it only takes a few new customers to pay for your entire direct mail promotion.

Determine the break-even point and develop a direct mail strategy based on these figures. By following this simple formula, you won't need a crystal ball and your next direct mail campaign should be a successful one.

Simplify the Purchase Decision

"Do you want to buy?"

"YES! Here's my money."

Wouldn't it be nice if all our sales transactions were that simple and that straightforward? No colors, sizes, or alternative methods of payment to choose from, just right to the point.

Unfortunately, life is not always that simple, and in today's marketplace, you need to offer options and alternatives. In fact, most professional salespeople try to avoid asking questions that elicit only a "Yes" or "No" response. If the response is "No," the door may slam shut, closing out any sales opportunity along with it.

Instead, a simple question of choice can move the prospect away from a "Yes" or "No" response to a "This" or "That." This is not a new strategy by any means, but it works.

Beware of one trap, though: You can go overboard with the options, alternatives, and choices you provide.

Twelve lovely products. Eleven fancy colors. Ten convenient sizes. Nine delightful finishes. Eight frequently admired textures. Seven gifts to choose from. Six bonus items. Five payment methods. Four shipping options. Three ways to package. Two kinds of service. And a partridge in a pear tree, with an extended warrantee!

By the time the customer is finished reading through a lengthy order form, he is beginning to wonder if he picked up a federal tax return.

People like options, and you certainly want to give your prospects and customers enough to choose from. However, make sure to give it to them in a way that is easy to follow and that makes it easy for them to respond.

Remember, you can always ask fewer questions on your order form *now*, and then call to obtain other information *later*. For example, an order form that simply says, "Yes, I want to buy," closes the deal to everyone's satisfaction. Then, after you receive the order, you can call your customer to ask if he wants things packed in twenties or fifties, or if he wants them sent in one jumbo carton.

The key to success is to find a happy medium. You need to ask the right questions so that your customer is confident that you can and will deliver everything you promise, yet you do not want to do anything that will cause him to delay placing the order today.

The Impact of Premiums

A premium is a gift, a bonus, something extra — something free. People are attracted to them. They like to read about them, and, even more, they like to get them. In fact, they like to receive them so much that it is very practical to expect substantial increases in response to your mailing just by using a premium.

But what constitutes a good premium? A good premium should be relevant and support your offer, but it should not be allowed to overshadow or detract from your primary product or service, or to be of greater value than your product or service. A free, stainless-steel cake knife in a Rosewood case with the purchase of a fruit cake is a darn good offer, for example. So if someone buys your fruit cake just to get the cake knife, you really have no way of knowing how well those fruit cakes would do, sales-wise, without the premium.

A good premium is something that relates to the same audience characteristics that your product attracts. You probably would not send a rock music cassette as a premium for a retirement home offering. Likewise, you would not use a windshield ice-scraper premium for people who live in Florida.

The very best premium is the one that has real benefit to the user even if it actually has very little expense associated with it. Think in terms of free recipes, a free list of the top 100 "somethings," or a free report on this thing or the other. It could be information you already have that would cost you little to compile but would be valuable to your prospects.

The purpose of a premium is not to overpower the value of your product or service. It should support it, help move the reader along, and encourage him to notice or act upon your offer. And, it is a win-win situation. Your customer gets a useful gift and you get the bonus of increased sales.

Reader Interaction
Increases Response

Scratch off the bonus prize. Stick the stamp here. Insert the token in the pocket. Peel off the star. Circle the number. Check the box.

Direct mail offers more opportunities to involve a prospect *actively* than any other advertising medium.

For instance, when the radio is on, a listener is often doing something else — driving, working in the garage, or cooking a pot of stew. It takes a lot to get him to stop and respond immediately to the commercial, regardless of the offer. Watching television offers a visual component to help hold attention. But most "couch potatoes" are not likely to jump off the sofa and run out to buy the advertised product. And, with newspapers, every advertiser depends on the same kind of interaction — reading.

Reading, listening, and watching are passive. However, scratching, sticking, inserting, lifting, circling, identifying, peeling, and marking are active responses to your message — *extremely* active.

The goal of this activity is not just to provide the prospect with something to do. It is specifically designed to help him *focus* on the message — to look at *your* message. Equally important, it is designed to keep him from being distracted by anything else.

The more involved he becomes in your message, the more likely he is to take the time to understand your entire selling proposition. By giving him a place to sign his name, a box to initial and a stamp to paste, your prospect very quickly becomes "dynamically" involved.

Think of it this way: These simple little devices that involve the recipient — the tokens, stamps, questionnaires, and quizzes — *drive* your prospect to talk back to you.

Even if you don't have the budget for tokens, stamps or stickers, something as simple as "check the red box" can be a positive interactive step. Anything that encourages your prospect to take a closer look at your company and offer is a step in the right direction.

Be Fully Prepared
to Respond Fast

Picture this: It's halftime of the big game (the direct mail campaign). The quarterback (your sales manager) is in the locker room (conference room). The whole team (staff) is present and accounted for.

"Okay, team," he (your sales manager) says, "we've got 'em right where we want 'em. We mailed a great offer. We've promised more than ever. We're priced better and lower than ever before. We look sharper than the competition. We've added lots of extra value to the deal."

"So, here's what I want you to do when they call," he continues.

"I don't care what it takes. Put 'em off. That's right, don't talk to 'em. Whatever you do, don't call 'em back right away. We're not ready to fill those orders."

Time out!

The point is that in many cases there is a correlation between the length of time it takes you to respond to your prospect and how likely you are to close the deal. An hour, a day, perhaps, is reasonable, but wait two weeks or two months, and your prospect is gone. How fast you respond to an inquiry, reply card, or phone call can make a dramatic difference in the final score of the game (sales campaign).

The best strategy is to be ready, even before you mail, with a game plan as to who will respond, how, and with what.

You certainly don't want to wait until you mail your lead-getting piece to start designing and printing your follow-up pieces.

Equally important, you want to make sure everyone in the company knows what the promotion is, what you are selling and at what price. It means being prepared to answer every inquiry just as soon as it comes in and to answer them with accuracy, professionalism, and precision.

Use Every Response Option Available

To encourage your prospect or customer to respond to your offer, you want to make it easy for him to do so. If he has to work too hard to respond, he may simply put your offer to the side and subsequently forget about it. That closes the door on any chance of a sale.

There are numerous response options available. Depending on the product or service you are selling, and the market you are trying to reach, some are better than others.

In any event, the one thing you absolutely want to avoid is assuming that your customer will be so overtaken by your offer that he'll run around, search out his own envelope, find, stamp, and then mail his order to you.

The following are a few of the most common direct mail reply options available. The key is, regardless of the response vehicles you choose, make it so easy that your prospect responds now!

Business Reply Cards and Envelopes

Preprinted postage-paid return envelopes and business-reply postcards cost you postage upon their return, but depending on your offer, this can significantly increase your response.

Return postcards are convenient for someone to request additional information, and they are also appropriate for orders when the method of payment is "bill me." Rarely, however, will a prospect actually return one if it means including his credit card number, visible to the world.

You can use this postcard-response option to start the ball rolling. If a prospect asks for more information, he is clearly interested in your product or service. Follow up with sales calls that will encourage him to make the purchase.

Or, if you include a postage-paid envelope, you can also include an order form. Your customer can fill out all the necessary information and return it without compromising his privacy. By including this envelope and an order form, you are letting your customer know exactly what you want him to do — to place an order now.

The best response vehicle is one that is simple and requires little or no effort on the part of your prospect. For example, plan your mailing so that you actually address the back of the business-reply card and then insert this into a number 10 envelope so that it is visible. (This serves as mailing information as well as ordering information.) When your prospect pulls the card from the envelope, all he has to do is check the box, sign his name, and drop it in the mail.

Whether you choose a postcard or an envelope, including a response option that does not require your prospect to pay for this response makes it easy and convenient for him to respond quickly.

Toll-Free Numbers

At one time, only the biggest corporations had toll-free 800- numbers. Thanks to the proliferation of private, independent telephone carriers, toll-free 800- and 888- numbers are within the reach of most businesses. Since the technology does not require special equipment, installation is fast and simple — usually just a matter of days.

You can use special numbers — seven to be exact — that convey your company's very special personality: 1-800-CALLNOW, 1-800-LUGGAGE, 1-800-CARPETS, or 1-800-BASEBALL. (Yes, this has eight numbers, but if you dial real fast, no one knows the difference.)

The bottom line is that for about twenty bucks a month and just pennies a call, your 800- number can open an important door to increased response. Since the call does not cost your customer anything, he is more likely to pick up the phone and place an order.

Fax Orders

Whenever you would ordinarily say, "Mail your order today," why not change it to read, "Mail or *Fax* your order today?"

There are a lot of advantages to orders that come to you over your fax machine. One is that you get the order in writing. Another is that you get the order right away. You don't have to wait a day or two, or a week or more, for it to arrive in the mail.

When you receive a traditional phone order, you have

to stop what you are doing, take the call, and talk to the person — *right now*. However, when a fax comes through, you can put it in the box with all the other incoming fax orders until it is convenient to process them as a batch. Your customer doesn't know that. He thinks you are already busy at work filling his order.

Fax orders are handy, too, particularly if you accept payment by credit cards or carry your own accounts. They also give you the customer's signature. You can never get that from a phone call.

By adding an 800- or 888- service to your fax machine, your customers can fax their orders without paying the long-distance charges themselves. This is particularly helpful if your customer does not have his own fax. If he borrows or uses someone else's or uses a commercial fax service, he does not have to pay the long-distance charge.

You can choose to include any of the above response options in your mailing. With all of them, you want to make the way free and clear for your customer to place an order. Anything that hinders his ability to act quickly and easily might prevent him from making a purchase. So, by offering various response options, you increase your chances of completing a sale.

Create a Sense of Urgency with Your Offer

When was the last time you received a direct mail piece that said, "*Don't* call now, *don't* respond now, *don't* order now!"?

Most people who send direct mail understand the importance of creating a sense of immediacy or urgency — of giving their prospect a reason to buy or act now. After all, that is what direct mail does best. You want to create this sense of immediacy because it forces the action, response or purchase to occur *now*, rather than *later* or not at all.

The value of having the sale happen *now* is that it increases the likelihood of a repeat sale. If you sell to your customer this month, he might buy again next month. However, if he does not buy this month, you have lost revenue that you may never be able to regain.

The following strategies help your customers and prospects overcome the natural tendency to procrastinate. They give them compelling reasons to act now, to buy now, and to pick up the phone and call *today*.

Use "Action" Words

Hurry, call now. You have only ten days to decide. Supplies are limited. Today is the final day. This offer will not be repeated.

Sometimes these terse little expressions appear almost trite — like throwaway phrases that do not really mean anything. But they really do motivate, because in today's fast-paced market, people are inclined to believe them.

Let the Graphics Speak

Words are not the only way to create a sense of immediacy. The design of the direct mail piece can influence the reader's perception of the immediacy of your offer. Starbursts, arrows, and reverse copy blocks say, "Hurry," in just the same way as do certain colors and the paper you print on.

Raise Your Prices

A price increase always attracts attention, but before you raise those prices, give your customers and prospects one last chance to buy at the old ones.

People are motivated when it comes to saving money. There is nothing wrong with coming right out and telling them that if they do *not* buy now, they are going to pay more later on. It is a sound strategy and it works. Just make sure you give them enough advance notice, along with ample time to respond.

Limited Time Offer

Sure, you may get an occasional order from someone you mailed to back in 1982, but for the most part, people understand and respect an offer that is extended for a limited time only.

"If you don't place your order before the end of the month, that's it! We'll never sell to you again." Too strong? Yes. The point is that you can educate your customers to understand that when you say, "Limited time only," that is exactly what you mean.

Supplies Are Limited

Even if you have a lot of inventory on hand, you can show it as a limited supply — a limited supply of last year's model or a limited supply at the old price. Make sure your customer knows that he may have to wait a long time if he does not act immediately.

Bonus for Ordering Now

We all like to get something extra. When you add value and offer a bonus, you may be able to convince your prospect to respond more quickly. This proven strategy has been a staple in the direct mail business for years — because it works.

Make it Easy to Respond and Buy

When you give simple payment options — *bill me, no payment till next whenever, 90-days same as cash* — you make it easy for your customer to say, "Yes."

And while credit cards are easy to use, they still require your customer or prospect to reach into his pocket, take out his wallet, pull out the card and write the number down. It requires more than simply checking a box that says "Bill me."

You can create a sense of urgency every day through the tactics you employ in the pieces you mail, which translates into more sales *now.* So, hurry, get out there and move your customers along.

Contests and Prizes
Impact Response

Contests attract attention. Big prizes attract attention. Attention leads to sales.

Contests can be powerful motivators. After all, who wouldn't want to win a new Mercedes-Benz or a trip-for-two on a Caribbean cruise?

Unfortunately, your customer already knows from experience that the odds of winning are often stacked against him. However, by including more small prizes, you give him more hope of winning something.

Prizes should be credible and have as high a perceived value as possible.

Sometimes, however, in order to create the illusion of a higher value to their prizes, companies make more out of something than it really is. They may call it a *professional home-cleaning system*, but when it arrives at the home, it is nothing more than a bar of soap and a scrub brush.

One way to test if a prize has value is to apply this simple question: Will it be retained? If so, it has value. A bottle opener, although relatively inexpensive compared to a Mercedes, may be retained and used. On the other hand, a jar of adhesive designed to bond glass to rubber balloons is probably not something that someone would find valuable and, consequently, not retain — even though it costs $300 an ounce.

Contests are governed by state law. Depending on the state where you live, and the state or states where you plan to mail, you may need to do some homework. Laws about sweepstakes, lotteries and contests vary from state to state, so it is always best to check with an attorney who specializes in gaming laws. For the most part, government agencies prefer contests that are fair and do not require a purchase to be made as a condition for winning.

While contests are not appropriate for every mailing, they can be a viable direct mail strategy. They work by attracting your customer's attention to you and your product or service, and that's the whole point of direct mail.

Special-Issue Stamps
Create Greater Impact

When you want to catch someone's attention — to catch him really off guard — *put a stamp on it.*

A fancy, special-issue postage stamp from the U.S. Post Office gives any envelope a personal look, just as though it has been handled one envelope at a time. It takes the bulk-mail image of your mailing and replaces it with a truly personalized appearance.

Traditional-looking postage stamps, like the ones that come 100 to a roll, are the most commonly used because they are convenient for businesses to use on a daily basis.

However, a fancy stamp on a plain envelope gets your prospect's attention every time. The really fancy postage stamps, the kind people like to collect, have the greatest visibility and attract the greatest interest — even if the subject matter of those special-issue stamps is not exactly your thing.

In response to the direct mail industry and individual heavy users of direct mail, the U.S. Postal Service is providing attractive stamps for bulk- or standard-class mailing. While they do not always carry the full impact of special-issue, first-class stamps, they can often do the work of their more expensive first-class cousins for considerably less money.

The Importance of Frequency

One direct mail strategy is so simple, so obvious, so important, that it can be summed up in a single word: *Frequency.* In other words, mail often.

If you mail 25,000 solicitations of one kind or another, and, after the dust settles, you see a profit, you can actually sit back and say, "This was a profitable business activity." So, if it was profitable once, why not do it again? And why not do it *often*?

After all, if you are covering the cost of merchandise, the cost of the direct mail promotion and any other costs associated with that promotional effort — and have a profit left over to show for it — that seems to be the perfect reason to mail more often.

Sometimes, though, businesses do not mail as often as they would like or think they should because they feel like it is too time-consuming.

That is exactly why you should use a professional direct mail company. As professionals, they can help coordinate all of your direct mail activities — a year in advance, if that is practical for you. They can make your entire direct mail program happen almost effortlessly and automatically, with limited effort and little of your time.

Utilizing Your Print Overruns

When it comes to printing, delivery of 10 percent more or 10 percent less than you actually order is a long-standing custom within the printing industry. If your printer prints less than you ordered, he is supposed to credit you for the difference. If he prints more, though, he is allowed, by trade custom, to charge you for them at a fair-market price. These *overruns*, as they are called, are the extra pieces a printer has left over after he finishes printing the quantity you ordered.

With today's technologies, most printers are right on the button. However, if any overruns are available, purchasing them can be an outstanding opportunity for you. With them, you can make copies of your solicitation freely available at trade shows, conventions, or association meetings. You can see that your dealers, distributors, and sales staff have an extra supply to distribute by whatever means are available to them. And, you can enclose copies with invoices and quotations.

If prospects ask you for a brochure, but you don't have

one, you can say, "I'll send you our most recent sales flyer. It will show you the values you can expect in the future." This also builds your database.

You can never have too much of a good thing — including the direct mail materials you print. And since the least expensive printed piece of the run is the last sheet that comes off the press, overruns become downright cheap.

Even if no actual overruns are available, ask your printer what it costs to run an extra thousand pieces or so. You may just find this an outstanding return on your investment.

The Value of Membership

Of the many things you can send with your direct mail solicitation, a free membership card can be one of the most effective. You can offer membership in your company's frequent-buyer club, or in your preferred-customer club, or any other "club" you want to establish. The key is that you want your membership offer to make the customer feel that he is part of a very special group.

Although the sales promotion and money-saving values you are advertising might be the same without the membership opportunity, by including it your offer suddenly becomes a special "insider" opportunity. It is seen in a whole new light.

A free membership card — or a trial membership card — in your direct mail package involves your prospect. By asking him to remove the card, to sign it and to put it in his pocket, he becomes an active part of your direct mail promotion. The more you involve your prospect in the material, the more likely he is to stay with you — that is, to read the entire solicitation. This is the kind of involvement that leads to an order, an inquiry, or a call.

In its simplest form, a membership card can be a part of the order form or the address card that appears through the window of the envelope. In this case, you simply print it on a lightweight card stock. Make sure to perforate it so that it can be removed easily and then retained.

It can also take on the look of a real membership card, similar in weight and appearance to a typical plastic credit card.

Another strategy is to issue a temporary membership card, good for a limited time. By doing so, you not only foster active participation in the mailing, but you subtly create a sense of urgency, which ultimately can lead to sales.

If you are able to get your prospect to retain the membership card you send, you have taken a great step forward in building an ongoing relationship.

Handling the Fine Print
While Keeping it Legal

Sometimes in a direct mail offer it is necessary to describe legally and precisely what the exact *terms and conditions of sale* are. This can be the fine print at the bottom of the page or those twenty paragraphs on the back in small print.

While you must provide terms and legal disclaimers required by law, you don't want the attorneys you hire to protect you so much that you inadvertently scare off every customer on the horizon by the overwhelming volume of legal text in your offer. This is not to suggest that you should sell dishonestly or do without your attorney and the terms and conditions of sale in your advertisements and order forms.

You can, however, be a little less conspicuous by putting them somewhere else — on the back or way down at the bottom of the page.

So, instead of having tons of fine print near where you want your customer to sign, include a sentence that goes something like this: "I agree to the terms and conditions contained below (or on the reverse)." Then, when he signs his name, the terms and conditions expressed in the fine print are neither staring him in the face nor are they standing in the way of his making the purchase.

When you keep the technicalities out of the limelight, you are likely to avoid losing the sale when your any-minute-now customer says to himself, "I'll read this later" — and later never comes.

Prospects Set Their Own Reading Priority

Look in the mailbox to see what is fun, and you will see what gets opened first.

Checks are fun. The bigger the checks, the more the fun. And tons of them are tons of fun.

Bills are not much fun, but they do get to the top of the pile of mail to be opened. A personal letter from an old high-school friend is always opened quickly.

People always open their mail in their own perceived priority of importance.

You will notice, for example, that people who are avid golfers, open advertising mail about golf before they open their monthly pension check. You will notice that people who like boats, will open mail about boats and boating before they open their utility bill. The goal is to get your customer or prospect to *want* to open your mail *first*, before he opens just about anything else.

One way to make sure your direct mail solicitation is opened first is to target your mailing accurately. That means putting the right piece of mail in the right hands at the right time. Golf mail going to golfers, not to boaters. It also means appropriate, exciting offers going to qualified buyers.

Another way is to design an eye-catching mail piece so that your mail gets *noticed first* and *opened first*. That means using the right graphic with the right headline — one that says, "I'm *irresistible* if you want to know about developing a better golf game, a longer drive, a perfect swing, or playing on more beautiful fairways!"

It also means educating. To be effective, your direct mail needs to educate, which means providing sufficient information to get your prospect involved and excited about your offer. Then, when he *is* involved and excited, he is ready to buy.

Teaser Mailings
Create Curiosity

Before you send out a primary mailing, think about building some anticipation for it by sending out a teaser. A teaser mailing tells your prospect or customer that something new and exciting is *about* to happen. It is a great direct mail strategy.

Teasers play on curiosity. They create a level of excitement, of expectation — even a positive mind set. Teasers set the stage for your future offer.

Be sure to avoid some inherent problems associated with teasers. If the teasers are too vague, they are not likely to be remembered or associated with the primary thrust of your campaign. Or, if you wait too long between the time you mail your teaser mailing and the time of your primary mailing, the teaser may lose all of its impact. Your prospect just will not connect the two pieces.

When your primary mailing follows the teaser mailing promptly, the prospect stands a better chance of remembering the teaser and relating the two pieces.

Keep in mind that it often costs as much to mail the

teaser as it does to mail your primary mailing. So, evaluate your strategy and timing carefully. You want to be confident that your teaser supports your primary direct mail solicitation.

An alternative strategy is to tease selectively. For example, tease your C+ and above customers, but not your prospects. Satisfied, experienced customers may appreciate the mystery, while your prospects may benefit more from a primary mailing that tells the whole story. That is one of the advantages of direct mail advertising. You can mail exactly *what* you want to exactly *whom* you want *when* you want.

If you like to tease but do not want to incur the cost of an extra mailing, use the space on the envelope. A message on the outside that mysteriously refers to the offer on the inside can create all the curiosity necessary to get the piece opened and read.

Make Your Customers
a Continual Referral Source

As you probably know, customers remember everything. They remember when service is good and when it is *not*. As human nature goes, good or bad, they are likely to let their opinions be known.

Customers are more likely to voice their opinions behind your back when something *bad* happens than they are to speak up loud and clear when something *good* happens. If their shipment was lost, or if they received the wrong size three times in a row, they will most likely tell everyone else before they tell you. Since customers typically expect things to be *right*, they are not as quick to talk about right as they are wrong.

However, if you know you are doing a good job, you can encourage your customers to express their opinions about you in a positive way.

One nearly effortless way of doing this is to include an extra mailer or catalog in your next shipment, along with a notation that they should give this to a friend, colleague, or neighbor.

Or, implement an official "sign-up-a-friend" program, rewarding your customer for bringing you new customers. Give them points, prizes, or additional products each time they come through for you.

Another way to keep your customers talking about you in a positive light is to keep the lines of communication open.

Ask them for suggestions and comments. Make them a part of your research and development department. You can send personal letters that invite a response, for example, or mail out surveys that ask a few open-ended questions and show that you are listening and not just counting.

Better yet, make them a part of your family. Personal letters of thanks or newsletters that are written in a personal and casual tone are great ways to build this sense of belonging. The more your customers feel they are an important part of your family, the more likely they are to build you up and refer you to their friends and neighbors.

Remember, the keys to keep them talking are good service and ongoing communication, so make sure that you provide both in abundance.

Postcards Produce
Powerful Results

Experience has proven that the postcard accomplishes a great deal and can save an advertiser a lot of money in the process. Because only one piece (the card) is involved in the mailing, you have only one piece to design, one piece to write, one piece to print, and one piece to mail.

Currently, the post office allows a single postcard, up to 4 x 6 inches, to mail at the postcard rate. Therefore, your card mails first-class for about the same price as bulk-rate, standard-class mail if you keep it to these dimensions.

Another advantage to the postcard is that because you have less to write, print and produce, it can come together quickly and cost-effectively.

Mailing a first-class postcard is a great way to check or audit your mailing list, too. With first-class postage on the card and your return address in the upper-left-hand corner, the U.S. Postal Service returns the card to you if it cannot be delivered, or if there has been an address change. Remove the appropriate names from your list and update the others. This is absolutely one of the most inexpensive, mailing-list audits you can do.

Another format is the double postcard which carries the same inexpensive, first-class postage rate. Think of this as two connected postcards. This format gives you more room for your offer, and includes a postage-paid, business-reply postcard that your prospects can use to respond. Including a business-reply postcard, with space for them to make a purchase or to request additional information, is another way of saying that you expect a response.

Whichever format of postcard you choose, be sure to design it so that it includes strong teaser copy or a powerful headline on the front, and an equally strong, right-to-the-point offer on the back.

Envelope Stuffers Can Ride Postage-Free

Every time you reach for a first-class stamp, you are looking at another sales opportunity.

When you mail an invoice, include an invoice stuffer. If you send monthly statements, include a statement stuffer. When you send just about any correspondence to a prospect or customer, take advantage of this extra opportunity to sell. If you're mailing first-class, just be certain not to go over the next ounce or you lose your free ride.

You can always find something to send. You can include something as simple as a business card, a Rolodex card, a letter, or a price sheet. A mini-brochure from one of your suppliers makes an extremely effective mailing, even if it features a limited view of your company or product line. Many manufacturers are willing to provide you with statement stuffers at little or no cost. All you need to do is to stamp or imprint your company name on the back and insert it in the envelope.

Another option is to create your own stuffers. They do

not have to be fancy to get the job done. After all, you are talking to established customers. Thanks to today's desktop-publishing programs, you can create a coupon, complete with clip art, in a matter of minutes. While the investment of time and money is minimal, the payoff can be substantial.

No matter how you look at it, it costs just one postage stamp to mail that invoice, stuffer, or letter. So, as long as you do not increase the weight of the mailing to over one ounce, why not include a stuffer and let it ride for free? Every time you stuff, you have taken an extra opportunity to sell.

The Power of Thank You

We all know that a "thank you" is important. It is a common little courtesy that we were taught growing up, but it makes a big impression, and, although the salesperson says "thank you" when he takes the order, the customer likes to hear it again.

Personally calling or visiting all of your customers to say "thank you," though, is difficult to do in today's busy business world. It is time-consuming and costly. You simply cannot afford the time or the money it would take to call or visit each of your clients after every sale.

But think about this. Mail is a very personal way to say "thank you" even though you can automate your message very easily. For example, the last activity in the order entry process can trigger customer service to send a thank-you note, letter, or card. Since they know exactly what the customer purchased, personalize the note by including that information: *We hope you enjoy your new Acme 2000 Widget.*

Or, once a month, sit down with your word processor and generate a personal letter to all of your new customers thanking them for their business. This is also a perfect time to tell them who they should call if they ever have a problem or need additional information.

While you are saying thanks, take the opportunity to mention another offer — to tell them about some of your other products and services. Just remember not to push. Keep it more gratitude than hard sell.

The cost of expressing your appreciation is nothing compared with the cost you might incur if you ultimately lose that customer and have to replace him with another. Saying "thank you" is a wonderful way to build a lasting relationship with a customer you really do appreciate.

SECTION 3

Direct Mail
Design

A Direct Mail Design Overview

In designing direct mail, many people have a tendency to be too concerned about the individual design elements. How does the headline look? Should we put a few bullet points here? How about some color over there?

Instead, try to look at your design as a whole. Literally stand back from your mailer and look at it as you would a piece of fine art. Imagine the blocks of text, the headlines, and various color blocks and photos as design elements — squares, circles, rectangles. Look to see what stands out and what does not. Then, consider the following points:

- Usually, one large, central graphic has more impact than a lot of little ones.

- Let your design direct your reader's eyes. The eye typically moves from left to right, then down to the lower left corner, then right again. Picture a big letter "Z" on your paper, and you've got it.

  The eye also moves from dark to light, from large to small, and from bright to drab. It always sees things that are out of place — unusual sizes, colors, or shapes. If you have six ducks in a row, all the same size and color, and all facing the same direction, except one, what do you see?

- In body copy, smaller type is actually easier to read than larger type. The old standbys of 10-, 11-, or 12- point type are just about as big as you ever want to use for running copy in the body of your direct mail solicitation. Paragraphs and sentences using larger type sizes make the reader work too hard. There is just too much eye movement.

- While you are at it, eliminate unnecessary color, visuals, and backgrounds around important text blocks. With the ease of designing on a computer, it sometimes becomes too tempting for an artist to "throw in" some color, just because it is easy to do. That extra color may hinder your ability to attract attention and lead your reader. Make photos and illustrations large. By cropping photos, you can direct your reader's attention to exactly the part of the photo you want him to see.

  You can outline product photos to remove unnecessary backgrounds, except where you show the product being used. Then, you want to bring it to life with a background that relates to your product.

- Keep your graphic elements in proportion to your copy. Words can lose their impact when they are over-powered by unnecessary graphics.

When you plan your design carefully, you can point your reader's attention exactly where you want it. A strong design improves your ability to communicate effectively. And, after all, communicating with your reader is why you create the piece to begin with, so you might as well do it the best way possible.

Your Mailbox is a Vast Idea Resource

One of the best resource tools we all have is our own mailbox. Daily it brings ideas — both good and bad — that can help you develop your own direct mail program.

Watch to see what you like and want to keep, and what you react to negatively and want to throw away. What makes you want to set some aside for later? What motivates you to open others now? More importantly, what motivates you to action now? Your choices often boil down to how well specific, individual details are handled.

What attracts you about the envelope? Is it size, shape, or color?

How does the way it is addressed affect your response? Are you offended if your name is misspelled or if your title is wrong? Does the type of label used make a difference?

Does a stamp impress you more than an indicia or metering?

If no return address or company identification is

evident, does not knowing who sent you the mailer affect or diminish your likelihood of opening it? Do you react positively to the style and tone of the piece?

The list of questions can go on and on, and there is no right answer to any of them. Your own responses to the mail you receive, however, can offer some clues to your own mail-piece design.

If you put your mail side by side with what is coming across your desk, and it matches up, you are probably doing something right. So, keep checking your mailbox daily. It might just yield the clue to developing a more successful direct mail program of your own.

Good Design Beats the Competition

When it comes to direct mail, your competition is not just the guy down the street who uses the mail to sell products and services similar to yours. Your competition is *everyone* who mails.

When you look good in the mailbox, your prospects are more likely to take a serious look at and consider your offer.

Today's consumers are extremely sophisticated. They all watch the same television shows and read the same national magazines and newspapers. They know what quality and good taste are, and they are keenly aware when it is lacking.

Good, clean design and quality printing appeal to those sophisticated tastes. In fact, you can prove it right in your own office by doing a simple test. Take half-a-dozen samples of advertising, at random, that arrive at your home or office. Line them up on the desk. Then, get a consensus from your coworkers about the quality and appeal of the pieces.

No matter how many people you ask, the preference will usually favor the pieces with high-impact color (not necessarily four-color), with a single, strong graphic and a powerful headline that gets right to the point — and clean, quality printing.

The point is you are competing for attention and readership among everything else that arrives in the mailbox on any given day. By increasing the physical quality of your mailing, you increase the chances that yours will stand out in the crowd of mail that the reader receives each day. This extra attention can only help you make a good impression and ultimately the sale.

A Simple Strategy for Better Design

With desktop publishing and computer graphics so readily available, everyone has become a designer overnight — or so it seems. Fancy borders, a variety of typefaces, styles, clip art, borders, and lines come right out of the computer and into your advertising. The ease of accessibility brings with it a temptation to use everything that is available.

Yielding to this temptation is fine as long as you do not try to use it *all* on the same piece. Instead, adhere to a simple design strategy called "**Choose one!**"

- Choose one typeface style for your headlines.
- Choose one typeface style for your body copy.
- Choose one style of border.
- Choose one thickness of line for boxes or rules.
- Choose one style of clip art, photos, or graphics.

Then, stick with what you choose!

If you decide to use Fritz for your headline, stick with Fritz for all your headlines and subheads. You may use Fritz extra bold for the main headline, Fritz bold italic for callouts, Fritz medium in all caps for headlines, and so forth.

Then, keep all of your main headlines in the same type size. The trick is to avoid bouncing around with a lot of different design elements. Be consistent.

Many of the best designers are the best simply because they show restraint and discipline by using and applying this same principle.

The beauty of this approach is that it is so simple. Try it the next time you do something on your own and see if it doesn't give you a more professional look.

The Value of
White Space

How much white space should you include in your direct mail advertisement? This is a tough question to answer because people either seem to like white space or they don't. There just does not seem to be a middle ground — no "gray area," so to speak.

If white space was sold on a per-square-inch basis, it might be more valuable and people might respect it more. In fact, they might even want to use more of it. Because its use is still debatable, let your product or service, offer and audience, dictate whether or not you need white space.

Some experts say that crowded, busy, jam-packed direct mail turns people off, and that a clean, uncluttered approach appeals the best. Others argue that the more crowded and busy a direct mail piece looks, the more appeal it has to the reader who is searching for a bargain, who has time on his hands, who has an affinity for your particular product or service, or who has asked you to send additional information.

White space is a funny thing. When you pay a designer

for a design, you see something tangible — type, headlines, photos or illustrations, borders, and so on. But when you pay a designer and he delivers white space, you do not always feel like you are getting your money's worth.

White space sets ideas off. It helps focus the attention of your reader. It separates one idea from another, and it makes what it surrounds look important. But how much does white space really cost? If you take one important idea, put it in the middle of the page and surround it with white space, and people take action or buy as a result of that design strategy, then that white space has paid for itself.

Be careful though, all white space never sells.

Keep Order Forms
Simple and Straightforward

Your order form may be the most significant *call to action* you can ever include in a mailing. Because, when a prospect opens your mail piece and finds an order form, he knows exactly what you expect of him.

As such, providing effective order forms is very important. They can be viewed as an ad within an ad, or a mailer within a mailer, and should be designed accordingly.

Design your order form so that it can stand alone. In other words, be sure to include and summarize all the basic elements of your full offer right in the order form itself. While you are at it, make sure the name of your company appears inside the order form, too — just in case it becomes separated from the rest of your mailing.

Order forms mean business, so resist the temptation to liven them up. Fancy, exotic shapes and screened backgrounds do not have any value here. In fact, they may detract from the business at hand.

Certain words work very well on order forms: *Mail Today, Act Now, Limited Time Offer!* They let your prospects know how important it is that they act now.

Make sure you allocate enough room to capture all the information you need. If the lines are not long enough or wide enough for your customer to fill out easily, he may decide not to bother with ordering.

Keep your order form easy and logical so that your customer wants to order now. Do not ask for information that might delay its completion. If you need to know serial numbers, birth dates, social security numbers, and so on, wait until *after* you have made the sale to obtain this information.

While you might prefer to receive the order form in the mail, many people prefer to pick up the phone and order immediately. So, go ahead and give them your 800-number, right on the order form. Don't forget to include a fax number, as well, for those customers who want to send you their order right away.

Finally, as a test, try filling out the order form yourself. If it is easy for you to complete, then it should also be easy for your customer. This exercise, will also let you know if you have omitted an important piece of information.

Remember, a well-designed order form makes it easy for your customer to place an order.

Envelopes: A Variety of Shapes and Sizes

Envelopes literally move the direct mail industry, yet most people are unaware of the vast number of different sizes and types of envelopes that are available as *standards*.

While the traditional Number 10 envelope, the announcement size, and the 9 x 12 catalog are just three of the most common sizes, nearly 60 different sizes of standard envelopes are available. For example, the standard 9 x 12 can come as a *catalog* envelope with the opening on the short side or as a *booklet* envelope with the opening on the long side.

Some little envelopes (designed for specialized applications such as stamps or coins) are too small to mail, while others are too big to mail unless you are willing to pay the price. If, with all the standard envelopes available, you still cannot find one that suits your fancy, there are companies that custom manufacture, or *convert*, envelopes for specific applications.

Different sizes and types of envelopes imply different

types of mail. A window envelope usually means a bill or a check. A greeting-card-sized envelope means you are another year older or being invited to something special. And, large envelopes add to the impact and perceived importance of the piece.

Envelopes come in many different colors, too, and the color of the envelope can say just as much as its size. Colored envelopes are sassy and rarely very serious, while standard brown envelopes denote something quite important.

When you want to reach the same target audience with the same message over and over, and you do not want to look redundant, change the envelope. By keeping the contents and message consistent, but changing the size, shape, color or look of the envelope, you keep costs lower while sending a mailing that looks new.

Stop and think about the envelope you use for your next mailing. Since you do not get a second chance to make a first impression, be sure to choose an appropriate envelope that will make you and your product look the best.

Plain Envelopes
Build Curiosity

Just about everyone wants to know what is in the plain, unmarked box that just arrived in the lobby. And people are very curious about the official-looking envelope that just arrived for the boss marked "Personal and Confidential." Wouldn't you agree?

The fact is, sometimes we can tell too much about ourselves on the outside of our envelopes. When we do, we may be actually contributing to its *in*effectiveness. Too much information printed on the envelope may make your prospect prejudge the value of its contents.

Most direct mail fits into one of two categories: *Overt* or *covert*.

Overt direct mail is used when you want to be up-front with your prospect, telling all there is to tell. Covert direct mail allows you to keep your identity a secret — at least initially.

If you employ a covert strategy, your envelope reveals little about you or the offer enclosed. Your identity is hidden until the mailer or envelope is opened. Perhaps the only identification is a small, inconspicuous post office box number or street address and city-state-zip in two lines — *without* the name of your company. In some cases, you can even forego a return address.

For example, suppose you mail a greeting-card-sized envelope, handwritten and lightly-scented with perfume to your hottest prospect. You put a fancy first-class stamp on it, and you purposely omit the return address. His secretary may hold it up to the light, sniff it, and shake it. But she is not very likely to open it — unless, of course, his secretary is also his wife.

The covert strategy plays on curiosity. A plain 9 x 12 envelope without a return address will almost always get opened. It simply looks too important to ignore.

When you use an overt strategy, copy on the outside of your envelope or mailer tells your prospect exactly who you are, what you have to sell, what the various key features and benefits of your offer are, and so forth.

For example, when you mail to existing customers with an easily recognizable deal, the envelope can actually help you get a head-start on getting your message across. "Save Big" on the envelope tells them you have a hot deal coming their way, and that they need to know about it. And even if they do not open the envelope now, they certainly should open it soon.

Should you utilize an overt or covert strategy? Let your offer and your audience help you determine which tactic is best.

Three-Dimensional Mailings Pack Power

Somehow, no matter what it is or how big it is, people cannot and will not dismiss or ignore a box or a tube that mysteriously arrives in the mail, without at least first peeking inside.

People know from experience that an envelope brings words and pictures. Even though those words and pictures can be clever, creative, fancy and even spectacular, they are still just words and pictures. But a tube or box, well, that brings them something big, something different — something they can hold and use, even display.

The mystery of boxes, tubes, and packages has power. Think of all the people who insist on shaking their Christmas or birthday presents before they open them. It seems like they would rather shake them than open them. Sometimes, just the anticipation and curiosity about what is inside is as satisfying as actually opening the present. Mail that comes in odd sizes and shapes arouses the same type of curiosity.

Three-dimensional and oversized pieces are especially

ideal for small quantity mailings. For example, if you need to attract the attention of the presidents of just a couple hundred companies, and you really want to make sure your message gets through, perhaps something other than a letter is the way to go. Even if the president's secretary opens the mail, chances are it will wind up on the decision-maker's desk if it arrives in a box or a tube.

One of the best three-dimensional items you can ever mail is a product sample. If this is something that can be done cost effectively, it's worth looking into. Nothing works like giving your prospect an opportunity to see, touch, and interact with your product. It may be the most convincing presentation you can give.

Three-dimensional mailings include advertising specialties, too. For example, if you send a pen, not only are you putting your name before your customer, but you also are giving him something to use to fill out your order form. Including an ad-specialty item relating to your copy gets great response and recognition.

Even if the mailing is not retained or acted upon now, chances are the ad-specialty item, with your name and phone number, will be kept and used. It also adds to recognition later. Just look in your desk drawer. Chances are you will find plenty of items with someone else's name and phone number on them.

While tubes, boxes and three-dimensional mailings are costly, they can be extremely effective in producing meaningful results.

Three Reply
Mail Options

Including a business-reply envelope or card in your mailing is a valuable direct mail strategy. It is an effective way to say that you are *expecting* a response from your prospect. Even in these high-tech times of order-by-fax and toll-free phone ordering, this familiar business-reply device says you mean business.

One simple reply option is to include a pre-addressed envelope that requires the respondent to affix his own postage. This is called a *Courtesy-Reply* envelope. A courtesy-reply envelope can be included with your customers' invoices leaving the remitter no doubt as to where to send his check.

If you use a courtesy-reply envelope in a solicitation, your prospect or customer does not have to hunt for an envelope and then address it, but he still has to find a stamp.

Another option you might want to consider is the traditional *Business-Reply* format offered by the U.S. Postal Service. In this case, no postage is required by the customer for the reply. As a business-reply permit holder, you pay an annual permit fee plus a charge for each envelope or card that is returned. This charge consists of the first-class postage rate plus a handling fee. (By the way, this is not the same permit as the one you may be using currently for outbound bulk mail.)

A third option is a preprinted or pre-addressed envelope with an actual first-class stamp already affixed in the upper-right-hand corner. This is known as a *Franked* envelope.

A first-class stamp on a reply envelope says you are serious about wanting a response. It is ideal when you are working with a finite audience and really want to ensure a strong response — such as with a survey or a for-customers-only promotion.

A Franked envelope has a way of making your prospect feel like he is part of a smaller mailing, a more select group. It costs more in postage, but if you're looking for response, this may do the trick.

Choose your reply-mail strategy according to your audience and your product or service, but by all means, let them know that you expect a reply.

The Efficiency of the Self-Mailer

It is not that there is anything wrong with envelopes, but sometimes it just seems to make a lot of sense to keep them out of the mailing picture. Instead, a self-mailer is often more appropriate.

Any mailing without an envelope, box, tube, or container is considered a self-mailer.

A self-mailer can sometimes be the perfect vehicle for carrying out your mailing plan. First of all, it is usually inexpensive to produce. Having less to print can add up to savings in production.

Plus, having no envelope can mean less weight, depending on what and how you are mailing, which can mean reduced postage costs. And, since nothing needs to be inserted, the costs associated with doing so are eliminated.

Besides reduced costs, another nice thing about a self-mailer is that it gets your prospect into your message quickly. When he receives it, he has no envelope to open and nothing to get in the way of your primary, dominant message — a message that he cannot help but notice. It is almost like mailing a mini billboard.

A self-mailer can be small. Something as little as a 4 x 6-inch postcard might be all it takes to get your message across.

A self-mailer can also be big. Something that is big when it arrives and then unfolds to a giant poster can be extremely dramatic and have tremendous impact. It can make one major statement, or it can display an entire product line.

A self-mailer does not fit every situation. For instance, a fund-raising campaign, soliciting contributions that require a remittance, would require an outbound envelope with a reply envelope enclosed. So, let your product, service, price, and target audience dictate whether or not a self-mailer is appropriate.

Unlimited Design Possibilities for Self-Mailers

Self-mailers are an art form in and of themselves. So, here are some practical and proven ideas for creating effective ones:

- Design your order form first. Keep it simple and easy to use. This helps you think through your offer for clarity. Remember, the less information you ask for, the less time it takes your customer to fill it out, and the faster he can order.

- Check your order form from a mechanical standpoint, too. Make sure you have provided enough room for your customer to write legibly and completely.

- Keep your self-mailer simple. Decide on *one* major objective you want your direct mailer to accomplish, and stick with it. If it is a free-trial offer, do not cloud the issue with bonus points for previous purchasers.

- Don't try to fit too much copy into the space you have. Too many words will probably not get read. Similarly, large blocks of solid copy set in very small type will not get read, either. Instead, use lots of subheads and do not crowd the margins.

- Using graphics tells your story faster. You can use many smaller ones to create a sense of high energy and movement, or you can use a few larger ones to show detail.

- Self-mailers are usually read quickly, so lead the reader's eyes graphically. It would be nice if all you had to do was mark your copy blocks 1, 2, and 3 so that your prospect would read in that order. Since you can't, move your reader from one point to the next with type size, color, color blocks, bold headlines, and layout.

- Don't hide your offer. Make sure it is on the front and back of the mailer so that it's not missed. Self-mailers should be easy to scan. Tell your reader right away what he is going to get when he responds.

- Make your self-mailer easy to read. A quick-and-easy appearance is imperative. More than in any other form of direct mail, graphics, type, and layout are critically important in the effectiveness of self-mailers.

- Use devices that involve your reader. Ask questions. Check boxes. Use piggyback or removable mailing labels. Whatever draws your reader into the self-mailer and keeps him there works in your favor.

- Finish and fold your self-mailer to an odd size. Try to avoid folding to letter size. It gets lost with all the other Number 10 envelopes. You may be better off going to 5.5 x 8.5 or 8.5 x 11 inches. It is even better to go with an unusual size that does not fit any normal pattern — just to stand out. The largest size that mails at the lower letter rate is 6.125 x 11.5 inches, and 5.625 x 11 inches is an ideal cut out of a standard 11 x 17 sheet.

Now that you have a few ideas to get you started, take out a fresh piece of paper and let the ideas flow.

Creating Effective Direct Mail Copy

Understanding the Communication Process

As our world becomes more and more technical, it is sometimes difficult to know exactly what the other guy is talking about.

The reason is simple. Communication does not take place on the sending or writing side. It occurs almost exclusively on the reading and listening side. You can write and chatter all you want in what you perceive as clear language. But, no matter how clear it is to you, if it sounds like a foreign language to your reader, you are not communicating.

Sometimes the people you talk to know more than you do about what you are selling, while at other times, your readers will have only a rudimentary understanding of the product. Since you may never really know the level of your customer's expertise, cover your bases by incorporating basic summaries and overviews in your copy that anyone can understand. Then, put the real technical explanations in a box all by themselves.

Your copy needs to find a happy medium between speaking to the experienced buyer and communicating with the prospect who knows almost nothing about you.

Avoid long sentences. Stay away from big words unless they are essential to your communication. Avoid jargon. Use easy-to-follow headlines and subheads. Recap what you say in short, frequent summary blocks.

Make sure your prospects understand your offer, know what they are buying, and are not intimidated by it. Unless your reader gets the message, all the tedious hours of selecting just the right words will have been nothing more than wasted time.

Understand What You Are *Really* Selling

While that sounds like a silly statement, what you are *really* selling may be very different than what you *think* it is.

For example, an aircraft manufacturer does not just sell airplanes. He sells fast, convenient transportation. The lawn service sells more than chemicals and fertilizer. It offers the pride of having the nicest looking yard on the block. Likewise, a boat manufacturer would not intentionally include a photo in a brochure of someone having a bad time on a boat. You do not buy the boat. You buy the fun, the prestige, and the freedom that having one promises.

In other words, you need to be selling the benefits of your product or service more than the product or service itself.

Sure, you may need to include technical specifications, but keep them to a minimum. Put the facts in small type, and emphasize the benefits by putting them in big, bold letters that cannot possibly be missed.

The benefits you project can be more important than

the product or service itself. Make sure you know exactly what you are selling.

Invest in
the Creative Process

Imagine opening a piece of mail at your home or office only to find a blank piece of paper inside — nothing else. Nothing printed on the front, no identification on the back. You do not know who it is from, and you do not know what it is about.

It wouldn't take long to see this as a complete waste of time and money on the part of the company who sent it to you. The point is, the most important element of your entire direct mail campaign is the message you convey to your prospects.

You see, postage does not do any selling for you. Neither does labeling, inserting, or collating. These are mechanical components necessary to make sure the mailing ultimately reaches its destination intact. They can never ensure that the mail gets opened or read, and they cannot sell.

Only *words* and *pictures* sell!

Using a professional direct mail copywriter may increase your production costs a little, but if a professional writer can help increase your response, it is worth the extra investment.

The same is true for graphic design. An investment in a professional graphic designer almost always pays for itself. Instead of accepting the first design you get, ask to see several. Even though you might have to pay for these extra sketches or layouts, the assurance of quality will be well worth the cost.

The point is not to overspend on your creative, copywriting and design budgets, but to recognize that when you invest in the *content* of your mailer, the overall effectiveness of your direct mail program increases.

Sure, you can write your own copy, and you can create your own design, but more often than not, a fresh approach — some new, professional, creative thinking from the outside — can give your campaign a real boost.

Actually, blank pages can be useful. They allow designers and copywriters plenty of room for creativity.

Sell With
Positive Motivators

The use of *fear* as a motivator in advertising and the media may be losing its impact.

You'll get sick. You'll lose all your money. You'll suffer. You'll finish last. You'll go bald.

These all appeal to fear — a warning of impending doom, a bad or undesirable outcome, or an unknown, negative future result.

Consumers are becoming desensitized. They want to hear something that makes them feel good. Try a more positive approach that appeals to their hopes and dreams instead.

You'll stay healthy. You'll make a fortune. You'll feel great. You'll finish first. Your hair will always be long and wavy.

Think about it. Which product are you most likely to buy? The one that makes you uncomfortable when you think about it, or the one that promises something better — a brighter tomorrow? Which approach is most appealing? The one that scares you and makes your heart jump a beat, or the one that makes you feel safe?

Direct mail is very personal. You have a perfect opportunity to create a positive feeling in your prospect's mind about your product and service. Something that is good, pleasant, and upbeat may stay in your reader's hands longer than something that is negative. Perhaps even long enough to be acted upon — which is why you send it in the first place.

Effective Copy Starts with a Powerful Headline

Headlines grab attention. They are supposed to pull the reader into the body of your copy.

Some people like them short, punchy, thought-provoking, and to the point: *1001 Great Headlines.* Others like long headlines. They feel that it is important to convey the entire essence of their entire offer right in the headline: *1001 Great Direct Mail Headlines from the Experts for Only $59!*

No absolute authority exists to say how long a headline should be. Your headline should be just long enough to say what you need to say to get your reader to pay attention to the rest of your offer.

Your prospect reads for knowledge, information or pleasure, not because he wants to work. You certainly do not want to hide your message, and you don't want him to have to work in order to figure out what you want him to know.

So, when developing headlines, ask yourself: Have I made a promise? Have I painted a mental picture? Have I created a sense of urgency? Have I explained how my product and service can solve a problem? Have I explained why this is an incredible bargain? Then, incorporate your answers into the headline.

Often, your audience will determine the type of headline you will use. If your audience expects you to present a serious, somber persona, make sure that your copy does so.

You should never ask a question in your headline that can generate a "*No*" or negative response. If the reader says "*No*," he may not read any further. And if he doesn't, he certainly won't respond. So be sure to ask a question that generates a "*Yes*" or positive response.

A "Three Reasons" Strategy
That Really Works

Here is a direct mail strategy that is as easy as one, two, three. We call it *"Three reasons why."* It is an easy strategy to implement. Simply come up with three important reasons why your customer or prospect will want to buy or attend, visit or enroll, and call or order.

Take a look at three reasons why this direct mail strategy works so well.

First, it forces you to take a long, hard look at your offer and program. It requires you to reduce all of your features and benefits into three concise, hard-hitting points.

Second, it allows the reader to get to your point faster. The faster he understands, the faster he can respond — and perhaps, the more likely he is to respond.

Third, it is simple. It works in just about every industry or business, and it is easy to develop.

Try reducing one of your recent sales promotions into *three reasons why.* See how this approach actually guides your thinking — from both layout and copy standpoints?

Can you ever have a fourth reason? Sure, you can have more than three. But when you do, you start to get away from the concise, make-your-point approach that you have worked so hard to create in the first place.

Can you have fewer than three? Again, you can have fewer than three, but do you want to? If you cannot find three reasons why your customer should respond, then maybe you should rethink what you are selling.

Three reasons why can fit almost any direct mail situation, so give it a try. After all, the three main reasons why you should use the strategy are simple: sales, sales, and more sales.

Establish Credibility
In Your Copy

Here is the single most important story you have ever read concerning direct mail. It tells all. It knows all. It is bigger, better, and more complete than any other story ever written. In fact, it is so strong and powerful that it actually makes every other story, textbook, and expert in the field seem insignificant, superfluous, immaterial, and inconsequential.

Sound a bit overstated? It is, but it helps make a point. Credibility is always important, but with direct mail copy, it is really important.

There are many ways to encourage reader acceptance of what your copy promises.

Start by adopting a tone that suggests credibility. Try using subdued language. This means minimizing the number of adjectives and adverbs. It means staying away from sensational, spectacular, captivating, and mesmerizing superlatives (there we go again!). Empty language draws attention away from the product itself, which can negatively affect credibility. Instead, use more nouns and verbs which allow your reader to get straight to the point and to the heart of your offer.

Avoid generalization. The more you explain in factual, documentable detail, the more reliability and believability your offer seems to have.

Quantify whenever and wherever possible. In other words, use as much precision in your offer as you can. Do not say "millions" when you can say 2.39 million. Do not say "hundreds" when you can say 1,295. Do not say "dozens" when you can say 128.

Additionally, be sure to use the magical words "you" and "your" as much as possible. More than anything else, these words link the reader to you and make him feel like you are talking *to* him, not *above* him.

Finally, use emotional appeals instead of logical arguments. You can build a strong, logical case for just about anything. However, that does not replace being able to look your prospect in the eye and tell him honestly and candidly that you have a good product, one that works, is fairly priced, and one from which he will really benefit.

Keeping Your Copy Exciting

How do you write with excitement? How do you motivate someone to pick up the phone, order by fax, or put a check in the mail to you?

Start with good, exciting ideas, not just words. So, when you start creating and writing, let it flow. Put as much down on paper as you can. Don't judge, evaluate, or criticize as you go. That has a tendency to block the creative process. Instead, just write.

Then, get away from it for a while. Never try to write anything in one sitting that is supposed to sell your product or service. You can always come back to it later, choose the good, discard the bad, polish, and edit.

Copy committees can hinder the creative process as well. They sometimes focus on words rather than ideas. Often, they are so focused on details that they miss the big picture.

There is usually very little excitement in the details. But in the big picture, you can spark the imagination and interest of your readers, which encourages them to take immediate action and to respond.

Copy committees are very useful in the editing process — checking to see that all of the bases are covered. Having a fresh set of eyes look over your work is always a good idea.

Professional copywriters can also help. Give them the details and let them develop the excitement. Or, forget the details entirely, let them develop exciting concepts and you fit in the details later. Either way, a professional copywriter can often bring a fresh approach to your copy.

Tell Your Prospect Exactly What You Want Him To Do

If you want your prospect to respond, you must tell him exactly what you want him to do. It is surprising how many otherwise perfectly developed direct mail pieces miss this point altogether. Don't be afraid to lead your prospect to your desired end.

If you want him to call, tell him in big letters. If you want him to return a business-reply postcard, say so. If you want him to write a check, make your message clear. And while you are at it, tell him exactly how much to write his check for — "Order all 10 for only $139.00." Or let him know exactly what he needs to purchase by putting a box on your order form that says, "Send us two dozen at the special low price of $159.00."

Perhaps you have received solicitations for contributions. Some say, "Please send money." Others are very specific about how much they "recommend" you send them. Or, they attempt to key you to certain levels of giving such as Patron, Benefactor, Lifetime Member, and so on.

When there is no reference about how much to give, some people will not give anything. They simply do not know what would be an appropriate amount to give. They do not want to embarrass themselves by giving too little, so they do not give anything.

But if you tell them, "Check one: $25 or $50 or $100," they will not be embarrassed about their contribution, and they might feel really good about how much they give.

The key is not to be shy. Tell them how much to buy or how much money to send you. Let them know exactly what you want them to do.

Keep Copy in a Conversational Style

When it comes to writing direct mail copy that sells and motivates, forget all the stuffy rules you learned in school. Instead, write the way you speak, using a conversational style.

Because mail is so personal, it calls for the same conversational tone and grammar you would use if you were sitting and talking to someone face to face or talking on the phone. And, few of us speak using proper English.

A good way to know what is right stylistically is simply to look at your speech patterns. What types of sentences do you use when you talk? Fragmented sentences? Yes. Contractions? Always. Short sentences? Mandatory and helpful. Choppy? Sometimes. The truth is that in spoken English and grammar just about anything goes.

Mostly, being conversational means being logical in sentence structure without forcing anything. It means choosing words that are "talking words" rather than writing words.

There are exceptions to the conversational rule. Most of these occur because of the product or service itself or because of the intended audience. A mailing intended to sell a new pharmaceutical to physicians probably needs a more formal approach than "your patients feel better fast." Many other technical or scientific applications call for their own vocabulary, style, and grammar. But even in these situations, lightening up the style can increase overall readability and effectiveness.

While you want to keep the style light, be careful not to send sloppy looking material to your prospect. Breaking writing and grammar rules intentionally can be extremely effective; poorly written text, though, can be disastrous.

Let your audience and the product or service determine the style that you use. If a light, snappy conversational style speaks to your readers, by all means, toss out the grammar book and give them what they want to hear.

Old Words
Communicate New Ideas

Many people are under the impression that new and fresh things are always better. The fact is, not everything needs to be new or different. Sometimes, old is actually better.

For example, picture the words "Revolutionary," "Radical," "Ultra," or "High-tech" at the top of the page. They are good words, but somehow, more than any other word, the old standby, "New," gets the idea across as well or better than the newfangled ones do.

Words such as "Now," "Last Chance," "Announcing," "Hurry," and "Amazing" have been around for a long time, but they are as powerful today as they were a hundred years ago.

In fact, these words act almost as a sign. Like a stop sign, they almost always get seen. They are recognized, and they are usually effective.

New copy approaches can be a lot less effective than the old ones. Look at this phrase, for instance: "Astounding Innovative Proposition." It just does not communicate nearly as well as the old standby, "Amazing New Offer."

The phrase "Concluding Opportunity" simply doesn't come out and say "Last Chance." If this is the last chance, come right out and let your reader know.

"Presenting," "Introducing," and "Announcing" are strong words that just should not be touched. "For your consideration" just does not have the same impact.

Is there really a better way to say "Hurry?" How about "Expedite your response today?" Probably not. That seems to take all the speed out of hurry.

Probably the best rule for selecting words for copy is to select the ones that communicate most directly. Use words that say exactly what you want them to say. Simple old words work just fine to communicate new thoughts and ideas.

Action Verbs
Overpower Adjectives

You want your copy to create as much excitement as you can. Color, big graphics, and starbursts naturally create excitement, but probably the most important tools for creating the excitement you want are the words you use.

Typically, copy that uses lots of "is" and "are" verbs has a tendency to be flat — not very exciting.

Take a look at the following paragraph that uses "is" and "are" as its primary verbs.

The book is 300 pages long. It is filled with facts, figures, and helpful information. In it are over 90 color illustrations to help you understand the subject matter. Plus, there are 120 graphs and charts to aid comprehension.

It is certainly respectable copy. It is clear, descriptive, and actually quite concise, but it just doesn't have any punch. It is not vivid, exciting, or action oriented.

Try beefing it up with some adjectives, keeping the "is" and "are" verbs. Maybe adjectives will help.

The handy book is 300 pages long. It is filled with dramatic facts, carefully-researched figures, and helpful information. In it are over 90 beautiful color illustrations to help you understand the subject matter. Plus, there are 120 comprehensive graphs and detailed charts to aid comprehension.

While the adjectives make it a little more picturesque, they don't add energy.

When you get away from "is" and "are" and look toward vivid action verbs, the copy moves much better. Excitement builds and your buyer is ready to buy. Case in point:

Jam packed with over 300 pages of facts, figures, and helpful information! Over 90 color illustrations illuminate your understanding. More than 120 graphs and charts impact your ease of comprehension.

Notice that even without the adjectives, the action verbs bring more energy to the copy — and in a lot fewer words. Remember, what you are after more than anything is comprehension, excitement, power, and action.

When you are writing direct mail copy, take a look at your product or service. Then, make a list of all the action verbs that describe it — action verbs, not adjectives. IS and ARE — that is, *to be, I am, you are, he is, it is, they are, he was, they were, I will be, he will be,* and *they will be* — are flat, actionless verbs. So move away from them. Tell your readers that your product "simplifies, purifies, activates in minutes, solidifies, replicates, empowers, increases, decreases, and separates the wheat from the chaff."

In other words, turbocharge your ideas with action!

Open-Ended Questions
Create Interaction

Getting off to a good start in a sales letter or direct mail piece frequently prompts the writer to begin by asking a probing or provocative question.

Indeed, questions are sometimes very effective and appropriate ways to begin a sales letter or to get attention on envelopes or flyers. Knowing exactly *how* to ask the question, though, is very important.

"How much do you want to earn next year?" This is the type of question that can certainly get a lot of readers to stop and think. Naturally, earning more money next year is something in which many people are interested. What makes it such a good question is that it is open-ended. It requires some interaction — some thought or mental activity on the reader's part to think about his future.

Resist the temptation to ask a question that can be answered with a "Yes" or "No." If the answer is "no," you may permanently close the door on ever making that sale.

For example, if you just ask, *"Do you want a free kitten?"* the case is all but closed when the customer responds with a definite *"No."* You lose any opportunity to show him the cute little black one with the white paws or the pudgy one that whistles when he sleeps.

Questions that pull readers in and get them thinking a little are strong and effective. *"Where else can you derive the pleasure a cute little kitten will bring to your life?"* Now you have him thinking about a furry, little, fluff ball curled up in front of a warm fire, or sitting in his lap while watching TV.

Questions that second guess and place doubts in the reader's mind are also extremely effective. *"Are you really sure your home can ever be complete without a furry new kitten?"* You cast just enough shadow of a doubt to motivate your reader to read on and perhaps to look at your proposal a little more seriously.

Open-ended questions force the reader to think and to put a little of his own personality into the picture which helps to begin a dialogue — at least mentally. Once you've done this, you are one step closer to making a sale.

Sale!
The Magic Word

One of the most magical words is *Sale!*

No matter where or how often it is used, it motivates, compels, drives, mobilizes, persuades, propels, stimulates, excites, quickens, and titillates better than a hundred other words. If you include this word in your direct mail advertising, it will cause the reader to look closely at your offer and maybe even to buy.

The word "sale" carries with it a promise of value and opportunity and the realization that things on sale are just as good as those bought at full price.

Sales are usually only for a limited time. That moves people into action *today*. Sales are a great way to get new customers and to motivate slow customers.

There are a lot of reasons to have a sale — Fourth of July, Washington's birthday, end-of-the-month, pre-inventory, fire, grand opening, moving, remodeling, and so on. The reasons do not have to be fancy, but they should be at least a little realistic. "Bored with my past sale" may pull for you, but its success is questionable. "Found my car keys sale" is catchy, but it is a little narrow for widespread acceptance.

It does not matter what a sale is called as long as the values are seen as real and believable by the customer.

So next time you send out a mailing, think about advertising some kind of sale. Come to think of it, holding a sale right now might not be a bad strategy for avoiding having to hold a bigger sale later on — a Going Out Of Business Sale!

Be Specific in Describing Benefits

Sometimes we have a tendency to be a little too general, a little too vague, or a little too obtuse when it comes to communicating effectively. But when it comes to creating copy that sells, make sure you get specific enough to do some serious selling.

For example, when you say, *"It saves you money,"* you are certainly getting across an important point. But be more precise. Come right out and tell the readers exactly how much you are saving them. "You save two bucks. You save $200.00. You save $2,000.00."

Or, if you say, *"It saves you time,"* do not be vague. Let them know exactly how much time they will save. "You save an hour a day. You save a day a week. You save four days a month."

And when it comes to specific features or benefits, the words "New and Improved!" alone are not nearly as dramatic as descriptions that reveal in precise and appropriate detail exactly what makes your product new and improved.

If your product is extremely technical, watch out for too much of a good thing. "Our newest model generates 215 megathrobs of differentiated gritzmeres at a base operating cataclysm of 42.51 turbobels when accelerated at .33 granules of a heck-of-a-watt per diminished cycle."

Too much precision can be particularly dangerous when you are writing to different audiences in the same direct mail piece. For example, very often, a single direct mail piece needs to speak to the boss as well as to the engineers. If you get too technical, the engineer may know what you are talking about, but his boss (the one who may control the purse strings) might not.

Rather than leaving out specific detail, take this approach. Include the details — megathrobs, gritzmeres, heck-of-a-watts, and so on — along with a summary of those technical terms using plain American English. Speak about benefits *everyone* can understand. The technical details allow the engineers to see the benefits of the product clearly, while the summary gives him something to show the boss. This approach not only communicates the essential points about your product to upper-level management, but lets them know that you know how to talk to them, too.

Copy Should Determine
Its Own Length

Someone once asked Abraham Lincoln how long a man's legs should be. As the story goes, he responded, "Long enough to reach the ground."

Inadvertently, in responding to this question, Mr. Lincoln may also have stumbled onto the First Law of Direct Mail Copywriting.

Put this question and Mr. Lincoln's extremely intuitive answer into a different context. "How long should direct mail copy be?"

Well, it should be "long enough to reach the ground." In other words, it should be long enough to be effective.

When preconceived notions about the length of copy come into play, they seem to work against the total effectiveness of the direct mail effort.

That means you probably do not want to start your creative planning meeting by saying, "Let's use a six-page sales letter." Instead, sit down and start writing. Say what you need to say. Then, when you have said all that needs to be said, stop writing. Your message tells you how long the copy needs to be.

If you allocate too much space for your copy, you can sit for a long time staring at the ceiling, trying to fill in the space. Not only is writing-to-fill-space not much fun, but it always seems to come out flat.

Believe it or not, it is more difficult to keep text short than to make it long. If you start with a preconceived notion regarding the page length of a two-page letter, for example, you may miss the mark. Not allocating the right amount of space can work against you just as much as trying to fill an extra page-and-a-half in your six-page letter.

So, when you are trying to develop the text for your message, just start writing. Make sure to communicate the ideas that you need to convey in order to get your message across. When you are finished, you will have copy that is the perfect length.

The Serious Business of Proofing, or
'Oops! Did We Prin That?'

Everyone knows that humor sells, but there is absolutely nothing funny about a typo. Not in a headline, not anywhere.

A wrong price, an incorrect expiration date, or a missing telephone number in your mail piece are enough to ruin your day.

No one knows exactly where typos come from. They just sometimes seem to create themselves. But attempting to determine their origin is not nearly as important or productive as finding them — and destroying them in their tracks.

Here are some pointers for developing an eagle eye:

Instead of just reading your copy for typos from front to back, make a check list of critical items that you need to proof carefully.

Check the headlines. Everyone assumes that they are accurate. After all, who would dare set a headline incorrectly? But typos can show up there as easily as anywhere else — there is no worse place for one to be.

Then, check the expiration dates. Check the prices. Check to make sure that you are consistent with style, capitalization, and format throughout your entire copy. Watch out for global changes. Today's word-processing and desktop-publishing programs will do everything you tell them to do — if you remember to tell them to do everything.

You may even want to read your copy aloud. Not only are you more apt to catch a typo or two, but you will also make sure that you have expressed yourself clearly — in language people can read and understand.

Read it backwards. Read it from bottom to top. Look at the whole picture, too. Have someone look at your copy who has never seen it before.

Most importantly, don't assume anything. Don't assume that someone else checked the final artwork, or that the typesetter, who always sets the type, set it and checked it. Take the time to proof the final artwork one last time.

(P.S. We know about the typo in the hedline!)

Keep Sales Letters
Looking and Sounding Friendly

Sales letters are not the same thing as sale flyers. They are more subdued in tone and style, and they address the reader directly and personally. Still, sales letters do not have to be boring or bland. By using some of the following tips, you can make a simple sales letter come to life.

Keep paragraphs short. The long ones tend to create a barrier. That solid wall of words looks like a technical report instead of a friendly opportunity.

Use underlines where they fit. Do not just underline for the sake of underlining or because you have seen others do it. The goal of underlining is to help the reader <u>read faster</u> and to help him get the gist of the message, even if he does not take time to read the entire letter.

Indenting entire paragraphs helps set off different thoughts and ideas. And indenting to a double indent moves the eye away from the left margin, deep into a thought or an important idea. But like underlining, use indenting and double indenting sparingly so the technique does not lose its effectiveness.

One or two lines set to the left margin with a space above and a space below, and using bold, underline, or all caps moves the reader along to the next major thought and helps him find it if he wants to go back to it later.

Using a different ink color for the signature adds realism. If the signature is offset or laser-printed, the introduction of a second color gives you the ability to add realistic-looking margin notes. These can be very effective when they are neatly handwritten and are used selectively.

The Power of the Endorsement Letter

Third-party endorsement letters are effective tools for advertising and direct mail. These are statements from satisfied customers about your products, services, or your kindness and helpfulness.

The endorsement letter as a testimonial of the quality of your products and services has tremendous power. This is particularly true when the letter comes from a well-respected individual or an authoritative group or organization. It is different from a testimonial that you include in your own printed materials. It is a separate piece of paper that you include with whatever else you mail.

Typically, the endorsement letter is written on the letterhead of the person or organization who sent it. It is signed by someone who thinks enough about you that they do not mind receiving a call or two to verify that the letter is really theirs, and that you are as good as they say you are.

The purpose of this letter is to increase the likelihood for action by your reader. It provides instant credibility because it comes from someone other than yourself. It is not your claim. It is their firsthand experience.

It is important that your reader knows exactly who is doing the endorsing. If you cannot get a "big name" to endorse you, do the next best thing. Look for a person or organization with strong perceived credibility. For example, if you cannot get Arnold Palmer, you may be able to get the Mid-America Amateur Pro-Golfers Senior Players Junior Tournament Association.

The letter may be written to *you* in the way of a thank you — *"Dear Acme Company: I couldn't wait any longer to express my complete satisfaction and appreciation...."* Or, the letter can address your prospect — *"Dear Fellow Americans: I want you to know that Acme delivers on everything it promises...."*

Occasionally, you get an unsolicited "thank you" note or letter from one of your customers. If you think it says everything you want to convey to new prospects, because of its genuine sincerity, then use it as is. If the letter comes close in sentiment but misses some important details, ask your customer if he minds if you change it a little. Most people don't mind when you do this. Some are even flattered at the prospect of seeing their name in print.

If no one ever writes you a letter applauding your company's virtues, you can write one yourself and ask one of your customers to sign it. You will be surprised at how many of your customers will say "Yes" if they do not have to take the time to compose the letter themselves.

The Three Most Important Words in Direct Mail Copy

There are three words that will never lose their effectiveness. The next time you develop the copy for your direct mail, keep in mind these three words.

You! This is probably the first word every fledgling copywriter learns in copywriting school. You have an opportunity to appear close and intimate with your reader — always referring to him as *You*. You talk to him in terms of features. You talk to him in terms of benefits. You talk to him in terms of his interests, ambitions, and desires.

You might be surprised at how many more times the words *we, us,* or *our* appear in copy, rather than *you*. By using these words, you shift attention away from the reader's needs to yours as a seller. However, by using the word *you*, the message is geared directly toward him, and you constantly reassure him that he is the most important prospect *you* have and that *you* understand his needs, wants, and desires.

Free! Like a magnet, *free* draws people to stand in lines for hours, to push and shove, and sometimes even to be rude. *Free* implies the greatest possible value, over and above the price of the merchandise. *Free* implies an openness that no other word conveys.

More than any other word, *free* invites your prospect to look at your product, service, or offer without making a commitment. Whether or not a condition to buy something is part of the *free* offer, your proposition can be seen in a very favorable light.

Free is an opportunity for you to reach a prospect who, by responding to your *free* offer, is labeling himself as interested in you and your products or services.

Free addresses a basic motivation called greed, which crosses almost all demographic and sociographic boundaries. Greed thrives on getting something for nothing, and even something of little real value may have high perceived value to your customer or prospect simply because it comes to him *free*.

What does *free* cost you? It might cost nothing, because every time you give something away *free*, you get something in return — an opportunity to present your story, and that moves you closer toward your goal: to sell something.

New! For a society like ours that is envious of anything and everything *new*, isn't it strange that we rarely see a *new* way of expressing that which is *new*?

No matter how many thesauruses, dictionaries or English professors you consult, you just cannot find a word that is any more straightforward or concise to convey the essence of *new*. When you advertise a *new* product or service, you offer your customer the chance to be the first at having it, or you provide him with the opportunity to do something different and exciting. People simply like the feel of *new*.

These three words have a proven track record. An easy way to remember these three important little words is to memorize the word *Eufreenu* (pronounced *You-Free-New*). Always remember that *Eufreenu* overpowers *Weusour* (pronounced *We-Us-Our*) every time.

Keep Your Copy
in the Present Tense

Much direct mail copy falls short of the mark by making far off, distant promises — simply by using too much of the future tense.

Our product *will* make you taller. Our concept *will* make you smarter. Our idea *will* make you richer. Our program *will* make you happier.

By using the present tense, you keep the promise and the payoff a whole lot closer to the reader — right here, right now, today! The present tense offers the reader immediate satisfaction, not at some point in the future.

Our product *makes* you taller. Our concept *makes* you smarter. Our idea *makes* you richer. Our program *makes* you happier. See, the payoff is a whole lot closer to where you are right here, right now.

In today's fast-paced world, it seems like tomorrow will be here before you know it. Or, it can seem like tomorrow will never come. But, the present has the most potential because it is here *today*, waiting for a sale, and ready to deliver on every promise.

A 10-Point Copy Effectiveness Test

If you have read through this entire section of this book, it is time to see if you're putting all these good ideas to work in your own direct mail efforts. We've put together a little test for you to take.

So, here goes. Pull out your last mailing and begin when you are ready.

1, Headlines are designed to attract attention — and to speak directly to the reader. If your headline contains the word *you*, score 10 points. (See how easy this is!)

2. As important as that headline is, the first paragraph is equally as important. It tells your reader about you, your offer, and how it is going to help him. If your opening paragraph contains the word *you* at least twice, add another 9 points to your score.

3. Advertising and direct mail copy have both features and benefits. The features tell about the product or service. The benefits tell how these features help your reader. If the copy is more

benefit-oriented than simply product or service descriptive, add 8 points.

4. The days of formal, stiff language are gone. If the language is conversational in tone, you are actually more intimate with your reader. So, if your language is natural and conversational, you get another 7 points.

5. Verbs can be active or passive. The active verbs — *go, get, put, jump* — are the good ones that keep your copy moving and your reader interested. The passive verbs — *are made, can be opened (or closed), is used* — are the verbs that tend to slow things down. If the majority of verbs in your copy are active, present tense, give yourself a solid 6 points.

6. Are you writing in the present tense. If your copy is free of the words *will, can, may, had,* and *have,* you get 5 points.

7. Go back to verbs for a minute. When you are using the passive voice, are you using contractions? Does *you are* become *you're* or *you will* become *you'll*? If yes, take 4 points.

8. Headlines and sub-headlines should make sense and communicate the essence of your offer, even without having to read the specifics contained in the body copy. If yours does this, take another 3 points.

9. The copy should be free of grammatical mistakes or unintentional spelling errors. If it is, add 2 more points.

10. Finally, take an extra point for taking the test.

Now, add up your points. Fifty-five points is a perfect score.

If you score between 46 and 55, stock up on order pads. Your responses should be pouring in.

If you score 36 to 45, you are producing exceptional direct mail, but some fine-tuning should produce even better results.

If you score 35 or less, this may be a good time to read through this section of the book again.

Now try this. Take one of your competitor's mailings and use it to take the same test. See how your score compares with his.

SECTION 5

Mailing Lists
and
Personalized Mail

The Mailing List versus the Database

A mailing list is a group of names — companies, addresses, cities, states, ZIP codes, and phone numbers. The information it contains enables you to contact your prospect by either mail or phone.

A database is all this and more. It includes a mailing list, as well as other vital information. It accumulates and stores as much relevant information as you can gather about prospects and customers in a logical fashion. Then, with this higher level of information, you can do more business and do it more effectively.

There is no end to what you can include and collect in a database. You can compile purchase history, color preferences, credit history, if they shop for the entire family or just themselves, if they buy only sale items, and payment preferences such as Mastercard, Visa, or American Express. And, you can even note how fast or how slowly they pay.

The larger the database and the more information it contains, the more segmented your marketing can become. For example, flyers about the shoe sale go only to those people who buy shoes. A private-sale notice goes to those people who always buy early in the season and never look at the sale price.

Every time you learn something new about someone in your database, change the database accordingly. When a piece of mail comes back with an address correction, note the change. If someone has moved out of your marketing area, you might want to remove them from your database. If they win the lottery, you might want to put them at the top of your list.

A complete database also allows you to personalize your mailing. Instead of doing an Anniversary Sale touting your own store, think about a Birthday Sale for your customer who is celebrating his birthday today.

"Mr. Jones, this is your day! And because we know just how much you love fishing, everything in our sporting goods department is an extra ten percent off — just for you — in honor of your birthday. And, when you come in, please stop by our manager's office on the third floor. He has a gift for you. No obligation, of course."

As time goes on, you can study your customers statistically to know who is *most* likely to buy and, more importantly, who is *least* likely to buy. This information can help you tailor your mailing accordingly, increasing your chance for sales.

Harvesting a Great Mailing List

The best way to know who to mail to is to know who *not* to mail to. When you stop mailing to the wrong people, your efforts yield a greater proportionate response, and you get better overall results.

Think about it. Through the process of elimination, you are able to remove those people or companies from your mailing list who have never bought from you, and who are not likely to buy in the future (based on your experience with them during the past months or years). Thus you mail more efficiently — and you save money.

It is nice to think that we are always mailing only to customers and hot prospects. For most mailings, it simply isn't the case. Look at those who never buy and never will, and remove them from your list.

Will your list get smaller? Yes. Will your list get better? Most likely. Plus, the better it gets, the more reliable it gets, and the more efficient your mailing program becomes.

Once you have weeded your list, it is time to start

planting some new seeds. Take the money you are saving from not mailing to the wrong people and start to grow another list. Do this not only with the idea of making it big again, but better as well, so that you see a more productive harvest.

Take the names that remain on your list — your best customers and really good prospects — and look for similarities — age, sex, income, occupation, location, hobbies, usage versus non-usage, and so on. Then, you can build a customer profile that allows you to identify prospects who are similar in characteristics and preferences to your existing customers. Once you know who these prospects are, rent a new list of names and start mailing again.

A mailing list is a dynamic, growing thing. The weeding and planting of new seeds (prospects) and their nurturing and cultivating is an ongoing process, one you will never be finished with. That is what direct mail gardening and the subsequent harvest is all about.

Clean Lists
Lower Mailing Costs

You know what it costs to mail a single piece to a prospect or customer. If you mail six times a year, multiply that cost by six. When you add to that the cost of production and printing, you see that you are investing a lot of money and time.

This simple calculation is pretty strong evidence that you want to make sure you are not wasting money by sending mail that is ineffective. To do this, you have got to keep your mailing list squeaky clean.

You can easily audit your mailing list whether you are mailing first-class or bulk rate. For example: Next time you mail at the standard-class bulk rate, print the words "RETURN POSTAGE GUARANTEED" on your mailer, right below your return address in the upper left corner of your mailer. Whatever is undeliverable, for whatever reason, comes back to you.

Then, take all the mailers that come back and remove those names of people who seem to have vanished, and update the records of those who have changed their addresses.

Since you pay for this return service at the first-class rate, plus a handling charge, if you mail something that weighs an ounce or more, you may be paying quite a bit to find out who is no longer there.

An alternative strategy is to mail a first-class postcard, which goes at a rate that is very comparable to the cost of bulk, standard-class mail. Plus, the postcard is less expensive to print than a more extensive mailing. If the first-class postcard is undeliverable, it comes back to you at no additional charge.

How often should you audit your list? The answer depends on how often you mail. However, it makes sense to audit your list at least once a year, perhaps more if you use it more than quarterly.

For instance, if you are getting ready to mail your biggest catalog of the year or an expensive campaign, plan to create and use this smaller, less expensive postcard campaign to audit your list first.

While you are at it, use this postcard to announce your *"New product catalog: coming soon."* Or, give the postcard value, such as *"10 percent off your first purchase with this card."*

The Power
of Personalization

"Mr. John Smith. We're pleased to announce that the Smith family may have already won a fabulous vacation. Yes, John, just think of it. You and your wife, Susan, your two children, Roger and Julie, and your dog, Spot, may have already won an all-expense-paid vacation. And since we know you're not likely to get the raise you've been counting on, you can't afford to pass up our offer."

Yes, thanks to better, more accurate databases and the laser printer, advertisers have the ability to personalize everything.

From fancy certificates that look as authentic as a Harvard Law School diploma to #10 envelopes that give rise to fears that an IRS audit is imminent, the consumer has seen it all.

Personalization has its place, just as long as it is cost-justified and effective. But the only way to know for sure is to send a test mailing — one group gets personalized mail and the other does not. If the non-personalized group responds as well as the other group, drop the personalization. Why pay for it if it does not produce better results?

If you still want to personalize, there are other ways to do so without getting so personal, expensive, or technologically advanced. Look at your target list and personalize by other, less specific variables or least common denominators.

For example, letters that begin "As a BMW owner..." can have just as much impact as full personalization, but at a fraction of the cost. Just watch your lowest common denominator and be sure. "Dear European Auto Enthusiast" is safer if you are not really sure about the BMW. But, "As a member of the human race" is a bit too broad.

Use Personalization Carefully

In most advertising mediums, from television to billboards, the advertiser speaks *impersonally* to an unknown audience. Direct mail is the one and only advertising medium through which you can speak directly to your prospect, *by name!*

"Hey, you" is certainly one way to get someone's attention, but when you call that person by name, "Hey, Fred," he stops what he is doing, turns around, and listens.

To make personalization work, though, you need to be accurate. There is nothing more unbelievable than a piece of mail that arrives personalized *incorrectly*. Receiving such mail immediately turns off many prospects. You need to do everything in your power to get the name right.

If you are not sure about a name or spelling, then you use personalization moderately. If you make a mistake once, maybe it is only a typo. You can be forgiven. If you make the same mistake a dozen times in the same correspondence, your error is blatant.

If you are working with your own customer database, you stand a much better chance of using accurate names when you personalize. When you rent a mailing list, maintaining accuracy can be a little tougher.

If you are not sure about the data you have, try personalizing your message in ways that do not rely so heavily on using the prospect's name. "Someone on Oak Tree Lane will be a winner," or, "A Memphis homeowner will win the grand prize," for example. This "generalized personalization" helps take the guess work out of direct mail personalization.

Once you have established a reasonable degree of accuracy in your data, try personalizing your mailing. It is a great way to get your reader's attention and to open doors of communication, which eventually can lead to sales.

Selective Personalization
Reduces Cost

If you are sending a large packet of materials, you may not *need to* nor *want to* personalize each and every component. Sometimes, personalizing just a single component — or perhaps two components — is more than sufficient.

Say, for example, that your mailing packet consists of an envelope, cover letter, order form, product catalog sheet, special pricing sheet, and return envelope. That is a lot of pieces. For starters, you do not need to personalize the envelope if you use a window envelope. This saves having to personalize the envelope and ensures the right letter gets into the right envelope.

Since something needs to be visible through that window, you could address either the cover letter, order form, or perhaps both.

Personalizing the order form is a good strategy because it makes it easier for the prospect to respond and for you to read his response. In addition, if you print a code on the order form, it can help you identify exactly which list produced the response.

Of all the components in the packet, the cover letter is probably the most personal because it carries an individual, one-to-one message.

As long as you are personalizing your prospect's name, address and salutation, why not personalize inside the letter, too? There is no reason why you cannot incorporate the prospect's name or his company's name into the body of the sales letter. Just don't overdo it.

By personalizing just one or two pieces in your busy mailing, you keep your costs down, too. Not only is the total cost of personalizing reduced, but the cost of collating and handling comes down as well.

Personalizing your mailing is a good way to get your reader's attention and to make him feel special. If you can do so while keeping costs down, why not try a strategy that may make your direct mail more effective?

Sales and Pricing Strategies

Look at Alternative Pricing Strategies

Save 10 bucks. One third off. Save 20 percent. These are certainly valid pricing strategies, but regardless of what you sell, sometimes it pays to get a little more creative when you are determining your direct mail pricing strategies. Creative offers sound exciting, which often leads to greater sales results.

The "*two-for*" or "*three-for*" strategy consistently attracts attention. Regardless of what you sell, it almost automatically sounds like a hot deal. Plus, when you offer a "*two-for*" or "*three-for*" price, you are indicating to your prospect that the price is so low that it is to his advantage to go ahead and buy two. In fact, this strategy is so effective that when you use the "*two-for*" or "*three-for*" pricing approach, you might not even need to use a comparative original or regular price.

Pricing "*two-for*" or "*three-for*" is a great idea especially when you have an item that is already priced low. It immediately encourages the prospect to think in terms of larger quantities. "Regularly $5.00, now *two-for*-$7.99" makes it seem that for just a little bit more, they are going to get a much better deal. You are doing better, too, because you have doubled your sale.

Most people are tuned into the concept of quantity savings. Quantity pricing — as in the case of case lots — is another natural for some things, like computer disks, photocopier paper, or wine. If the product is consumed in one way or another, a great deal can be gained by both buyer and seller if quantity pricing is used.

Another pricing structure that is sure to encourage a larger sale is to use the word *"free."* There is nothing like that old word *"free"* to motivate. "Purchase ten boxes, get another *free."* Again, the buyer gets a better deal and you increase your sales.

One pricing strategy used effectively by magazine publishers and membership organizations is prepaid annual subscriptions. This strategy is often overlooked. Many products and services can be arranged into an annual quantity and sold a year in advance.

For example, there are six days during the year in which someone is inclined to purchase flowers: *Valentine's Day, Easter, Mother's Day, Christmas, Spouse's Birthday, and Wedding Anniversary.* If the average amount spent per occasion is $30.00, a shrewd florist can offer an annual floral program for $179.00. As a member of this program, you receive an appropriate arrangement on each occasion.

The price is the same as purchasing each arrangement on the day of the occasion, however, the customer does not have to remember to place the order. In many cases, the convenience is worth the advance payment.

In today's marketplace, people are always on the lookout for something different, especially when it comes to pricing, so don't use all of your creativity in designing the mailing. Save some of it for establishing a creative pricing strategy, as well.

Price and Quality
Establish True Value

Value is a perception of how a buyer sees the relationship between price and quality as it relates to services or products. Sure, finding a low price is important, but many of today's consumers don't just want the cheapest product. In fact, they may be instinctively reluctant to trust the lowest-priced product simply because it *is* the lowest. Without value, price means practically nothing.

So in your direct mail efforts, make sure to emphasize the value of your offer. Demonstrate how the product you are selling today is better than the one you were selling just a few short years ago. Talk about longer, more comprehensive warranties as a result of these improvements. Talk about new designs, current research, state-of-the-art technology, and so on.

Graphically compare your product to the competition. To be effective, these cannot be simply claims or allegations. Accompany your comparisons with meaningful charts, photos, graphs — hard data!

Show price as cost per day, cost per week, and cost per

usage. Show price as it relates to a portion of the whole of their business or home activities. Show price as it relates to length of ownership.

More than anything, today's consumer wants to feel as though he has obtained a super deal — that he got the most, the best, the biggest, and the most reliable — for his money. He also wants to consider himself a smart shopper.

Don't Chop Price, Add Value!

One way to attract buyers is to lower prices, but if sales are slow and margins seem tighter than ever, this can hurt. Instead, try to attract buyers by adding value. Give your prospect more for his money rather than by taking cuts yourself. You can frequently add value without it actually costing you anything.

Suppose you sell boxes of marbles all day at $99.95, but your competition keeps lowering their price. Eventually, their's is down to $78.95, which is hard to beat. Why keep pace by giving the store away?

Instead of cutting your prices, try adding some value. Offer your customer a free designer bag for the marbles when they purchase them at your regular price. Let's say you usually charge $9.55 for this fancy bag and your cost is $4.95. By giving away the bag you have added $10.00 of value with a cost of only $5.00 dollars, a lot less pain than giving up $10.00 of your retail.

Throw in free gift wrapping, pointing out that you normally charge $9.95 for it (these are big marbles!).

Stop and compute the math. So far, you are giving about 20 percent more value to your marbles than the competitor — even though you are selling them for full price.

There's even more you can add. Include a coupon for an extra 10 percent off their next purchase of marbles, and you will help bring your customers back to you. If they buy the next time, it only costs you five percent off this first sale, and five percent off the next. When you include a free marble polishing rag that usually sells for $6.95, but that you get for free, the perceived value of your product increases incredibly.

You don't want to give your product away, but by adding value, you may be able to attract attention and make or retain a customer. Most importantly, you stand a better chance of keeping some profit in the deal.

So leave the price-chopping to your competition. By adding value, you can maintain a solid bottom line without "losing your marbles" over price cutting.

Compare Price
to Familiar Things

The heart of much direct mail is pricing. How much does your product or service cost, or how much can your prospect save? Advertising a savings of ten or twenty bucks or ten or twenty percent, communicates precisely what your offer is, or how much your prospect can save. However, you can use a better way to demonstrate dramatically how affordable and exciting your offer is.

Instead of advertising a price of "only $12.95," relate the cost of your product or service to something that your prospect already knows, something he is already very familiar with. For instance, "For about what you'd spend for a steak dinner, you get..."

People can relate to what a steak dinner costs (especially those who can still afford one). If they remember their last steak dinner at $7.95, that makes their perception of your deal even better. If they remember their last steak dinner at $19.95, they may have a very different perception.

You need to be careful about what you use for comparative pricing. You always want to keep comparatives within the day-to-day frame of reference of your prospects.

By approaching pricing in a comparative rather than direct approach, your product or service is seen as being close and accessible to your prospect and more embraceable because it is already within their frame of reference.

Use Every Response as an Opportunity to Sell

When you mail, you are bound to get response. Some people will buy, and some will not. Think about it this way. Direct mail is just like fishing. Some bite, some get away.

Those who take your bait become likely candidates to buy more. As customers, they suddenly become very receptive to hearing more about your products and services. They not only listen to your advice, they may actually go out of their way to seek it.

When you get a new customer, try to *up-sell*. In other words, try to sell him more. Established customers always make the best prospects to *up-sell*, but the interesting thing is that it does not seem to make much difference if they are happy customers or not. The possibility to *up-sell* exists either way.

Case in point: To the happy customer, you say, "If you like the basic pack, buy the expanded pack. You'll enjoy its added features." To the unhappy customer, you say, "If you're having trouble with the basic pack, buy the expanded pack. That's what the people do who get the most enjoyment out of the basic pack." Either way, you have made the most of an existing customer relationship.

But what about those who don't buy? After all, they make up the majority of the prospects you mail to. For the ones who get away, you may need to change the bait, to down sell just a bit.

Start with price, for example. If they see your offer as a really good deal, they may buy it. These new customers can then be treated to an *up-sell*.

Each time you mail, you sell some. Take the ones you sell, put them in the group with all the other customers, and *up-sell*. Treat them as preferred customers. To those you do not catch, mail again. This time, reduce the minimum quantity or change the structure of the offer itself. Offer different bait each time, and eventually they might bite.

Each time you send out a mailing, think of it as casting a line. With a little patience and the right bait, you should be reeling in the sales before you know it.

Send No Money!
We'll Bill You Later

Sometimes, no matter how much you would like to say, "Send your money now (because we really need it!)," it makes a lot more sense to separate the payment for goods or services from the initial decision and commitment to purchase.

You see this strategy all the time with magazine subscriptions and renewals. You see it for trade show and seminar registrations, too. They want to get you so emotionally excited about what they have to offer that you will jump at their opportunity now. After all, their product or service is something you want and need, so if you do not have to pay for it now, why wouldn't you commit?

The advantage to this strategy is that when you keep the emotional decision to buy separate from asking your prospect to reach for his wallet, you stand the chance of booking more business.

One reason that this strategy works so well — particularly for magazines, trade shows, and educational seminars — is that the marginal cost to provide these goods or services to an additional person is relatively low. As such, any loss they might incur from nonpayment would be very low.

The "bill me later" strategy adds credibility to your offer and to your company. You project an air of trust. After all, if you are confident enough to bill your customers after you make the sale, you must have a very high level of customer satisfaction.

While this strategy may not be appropriate for personalized merchandise or for larger ticket items that have a high cost associated with them, you can still use the "bill me later" concept. No one says that you have to ship the merchandise before you actually receive payment. You are only saying, "We'll bill you later." So, ask for the order now. When you receive the order, you invoice. Then, when you receive payment, you ship.

As a sales strategy, "bill me later" works wonders. Remember, good things come to those who wait.

Guarantees Encourage Prospects to Buy

Guarantees help reinforce the fact that your company is a *good* company, that your product is sound, and that you deliver exactly what you promise. They are particularly important when you are attempting to attract new business.

Think about what a guarantee does for you when you are the purchaser. It eliminates your risk in purchasing. It invites you to try something without having to make an irrevocable buying decision. Being able to buy with such confidence might open the door for you to become a steady, repeat customer.

Naturally, you want to word your guarantee precisely. Do not leave any question or doubt in your prospect's mind regarding exactly what is being guaranteed and for how long. Also, refer to and reinforce your guarantee wherever and whenever you can, in your cover letter, in your brochure, and in your sales presentation. Your guarantee is only important to your prospect if it is important to you.

Guarantees can get a little tricky and technical because of federal and state regulations, so be sure to work with an attorney who is well-versed in drafting guarantees. Official, legal guarantees can get a little long-winded, so for your customers, be sure to translate any technical verbiage from a lengthy and complicated guarantee into a few, well-chosen words. "Complete money-back guarantee" condenses the essence of even the most lengthy and complicated guarantee.

The longer your guarantee is in effect, the more likely your customer is to *forget* that he has a guarantee in the first place. For instance, if you give someone a 10-day guarantee on a new pair of drumsticks, they will very likely grab those sticks and beat on everything in sight — looking for a flaw and a reason to return them. But if you give them a 12-month guarantee, it may take months for them to get into the rhythm of those sticks — let alone to remember the unconditional money-back guarantee.

Guarantees don't have to be money-back guarantees in order to be effective. *Guaranteed next day shipping, guaranteed lowest price,* even *guaranteed best guarantee* can be equally effective and help differentiate you from your competition.

Whatever your guarantee, once you communicate it to your prospects, you are guaranteed to see results.

A Simple Strategy for Generating Sales and Cash

Even when sales are brisk, money can sometimes lag far behind the actual sale. Some simple strategies for selling can be very attractive to your customers while, at the same time, help you to raise funds.

For example, you might send out a direct mail piece that says, "Because of our special low pricing, we can't ship these promotional items on open account or for later payment. Please enclose your payment now to take advantage of this one-time offer."

The logic behind this approach is that when you are offering as much as you are through discounts, bonuses, additional product and added value, you have the right to ask for faster payment. This rationale actually makes a great deal of sense to your prospects and customers who are looking for a deal. The lower price means more to them than longer terms.

Thanks to United Parcel Service and Federal Express, shipping C.O.D. is faster and easier than ever before. They arrive the next day and say, "Here are the goods, now give us the money." While it sounds harsh, it may be acceptable to even your best customers when they see the benefit of a special deal.

Better Listening
Leads to Better Selling

Every person who responds to your direct mail offer is a potential sale. Yet, many times these inquiries are lost, (forever), because people are not trained to listen to what our prospects are really saying.

For example, you advertise "black only." It is printed in the flyer, really big. In fact, no one can miss it. Then the first call comes in and your sales person answers the phone. The voice on the line asks, "Does it come in any other color?"

If the sales person replies, "*Sorry, no,*" the caller hangs up, ending any chance for you to sell the product to him.

That answer just cost you a lot of money — not just in the lost sale, but in the cost of bringing that prospect to you.

If, to the same question, the sales person instead responds, "*Does that present a problem for you?*" — then a dialogue begins. The sales person can discover why the prospect thinks black would be undesirable or unsuitable. Then, the salesperson can explain to the prospect that black goes with anything, that it can be painted as a do-it-yourself project, that black makes people look thinner, that it is hardly seen once it is installed, and the objections seem to vanish.

Thorough sales training and briefings to everyone who gets anywhere near a customer, personally or by phone, can be one of the most important strategies you employ to maximize the effectiveness of your direct mail program.

Reposition Products for Increased Sales

Sometimes you can bring a fresh approach to your mailings by looking at your product and service from a narrowly targeted, or market niche, standpoint. You do not actually change your product. You simply change the way you position it and market it to each of your target markets.

What you are doing, in effect, is taking your product "as is" and making it "look" specific for a given industry or market segment. You position yourself as a *specialized* provider as opposed to a *general* provider, and you build your direct mail solicitation accordingly.

Suppose you manufacture No. 2 wood pencils. Most people think that a No. 2 pencil is just a No. 2 pencil. But when you mail to elementary schools, you can market that ordinary No. 2 pencil as *"the ultimate No. 2 pencil for children learning to write."* Or, when you mail to engineers and drafting firms, you can advertise that same No. 2 pencil as *"the world's sharpest No. 2 pencil for drafting."* Get the point?

All you need to execute this powerful strategy is a new cover on your catalog or different teaser copy on the outside of your envelope to open up a whole new market for your products.

Even more interesting is that sometimes the smaller the niche, the better. How about a No. 2 pencil specially balanced for people who wear them behind their ear? Or a No. 2 pencil for space travel? The government might pay millions for that.

The bonus is that sometimes these niche markets can give you higher margins because your product is seen as specific to the given audience rather than generic.

Look for the various ways you can position your product so that it speaks directly to your audience. That audience might just speak back directly to you — through an abundance of new sales.

Sell More
Than One

It's simple mathematics. If you know that your advertising and direct mail costs are relatively fixed, that your response rate is usually always about the same, and that your gross margin percentage is constant most of the time, then you also know that a $100.00 order produces more contribution to profit than a $20.00 order. Even without a calculator, it looks like about five times more!

So, it makes sense to push the size of the order up – to sell two instead of one, twelve instead of ten, a gross instead of a hundred.

This strategy may be easier than you think. Sometimes, simply repackaging the way you approach and sell your product is all that it takes. It's called "unitizing." Taking single items and putting them together into a single unit. Cola used to be sold one bottle at a time, then came the six-pack and twelve-pack, followed, of course, by the eight-pack, and in some places, the four-pack.

Repackaging doesn't always have to mean putting things in a box or carton. It simply means presenting products in a different light — giving your customers and prospects strong, compelling reasons to buy more, and to buy those larger quantities right now.

Special promotions are an ideal way to encourage larger orders. End-of-season clearances, anniversary sales, introductory specials, case-load sales, warehouse clearances, and so on are all natural reasons to encourage prospects to buy more now.

Naturally, you can always increase contribution to profit by raising prices on single units. While this may be practical for some items, for others it simply won't work. The market is what the market will bear.

However, by working to increase the number of units you sell per order, you have the potential to increase sales by a significant multiple.

For example, if your customers always buy three at a time, and through strong, direct mail marketing you are able to motivate them to buy six at a time, you've instantly doubled the size of your business. Now that's a powerful reason for thinking about selling more than one at a time.